GUITAR STUDIES IN IMPROVISATION

An introduction to scales, chords
and progression studies,
that can be used for
improvisation.

By Ambrose Rivera
and Richard D. Wartick

P.O. Box 814
Cedar Crest, NM 87008
505-281-5060

PREFACE

To play an improvised melody, find the key, work the scales (modes) and arpeggios (chord tones) with respect to melodic form. In effect, what we are doing is composing a song spontaneously. Indeed, a composer begins by putting notes together (improvising) then eventually develops into a finished melody, at which time the improvisation becomes a composition. So, improvisation can be thought of as that first step in composition.

The following study explores these tonal resources, (scales chords and progressions) in several common keys. The study is written in traditional notation, tablature and diagram form. For a complete reference book of all keys, see us about MUSIC THEORY IN ALL KEYS FOR GUITAR.

A CD may be purchased from Amazon, which includes all of the accompanying tracks as referenced in Guitar Studies In Improvisation.

Enjoy!

Ambrose Rivera

Teacher Author Performer

CONTENTS

The Pentatonic Scale
Key Of Amin

Guitar Licks

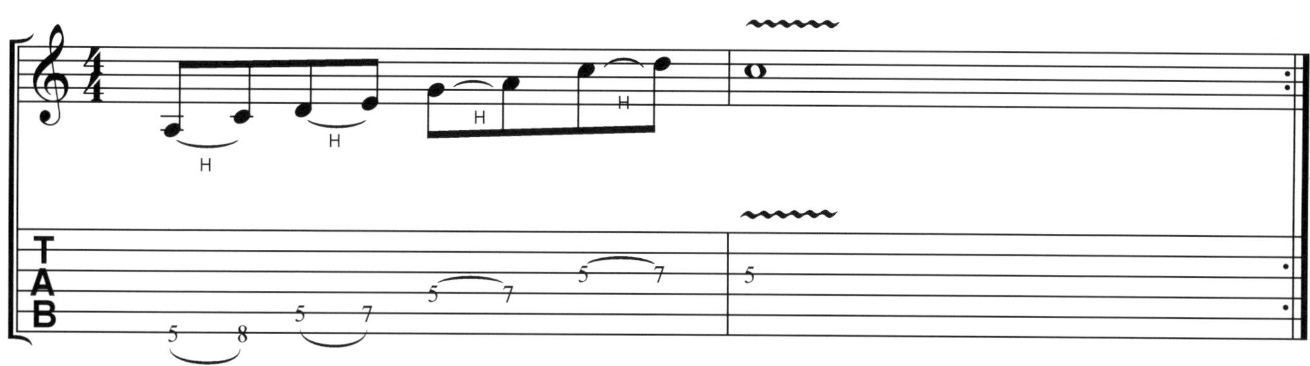

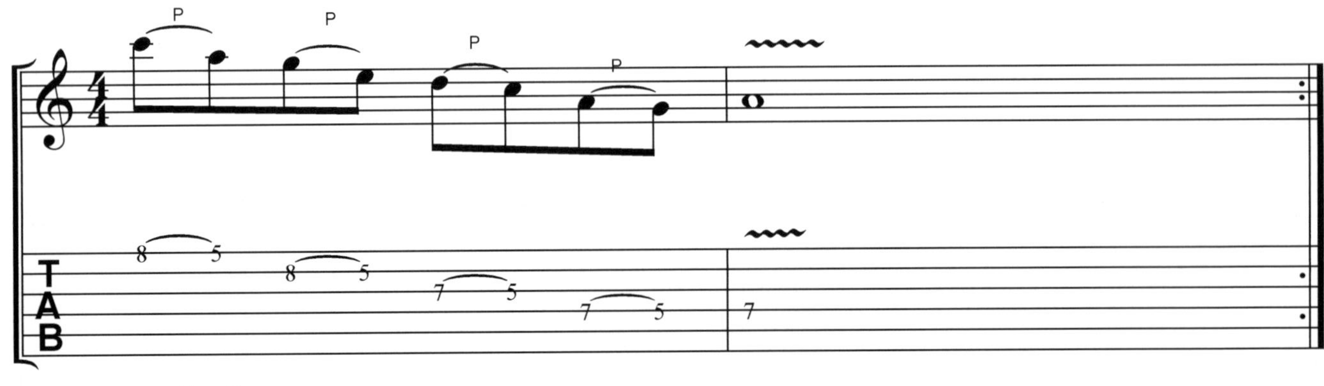

Pull-offs

Slides

Use these 2 measure licks to inspire your own ideas.

Latin Rock

The following changes (progressions) are found in many songs. Listen carefully and many will come to mind.

Improvise a melody using the Amin pentatonic scale over all of these chord changes.

12 Bar Blues

A 7
5fr.
Track 3
D 7
3fr.
A 7
5fr.
E 7
5fr.
D 7
3fr.
A 7
5fr.
E 7
5fr.
A 7
5fr.
1.
2.

Scale Studies
Amin Pentatonic

These are 5 different patterns at 5 positions on the fingerboard. Memorize them all and learn to shift from one to another.

As you can see these five patterns at 5 positions on the fingerboard extend the range of the scale up the neck. Learn to identify them by pattern number and reference chord.

Blues Licks in A

Play these licks as pieces of musical themes, then play your own variations.

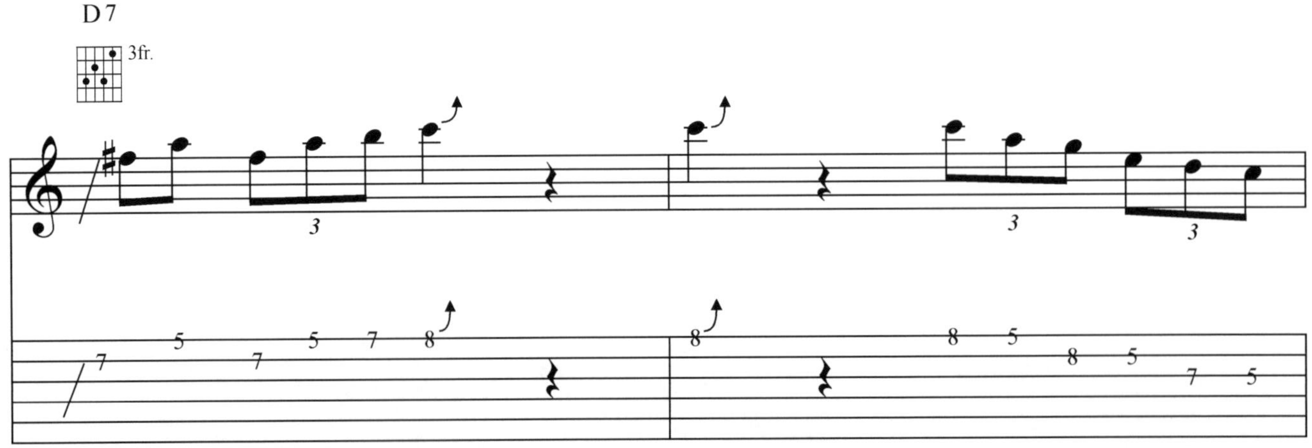

A 7
5fr.
3
7
5
7
5
7
5
7
7

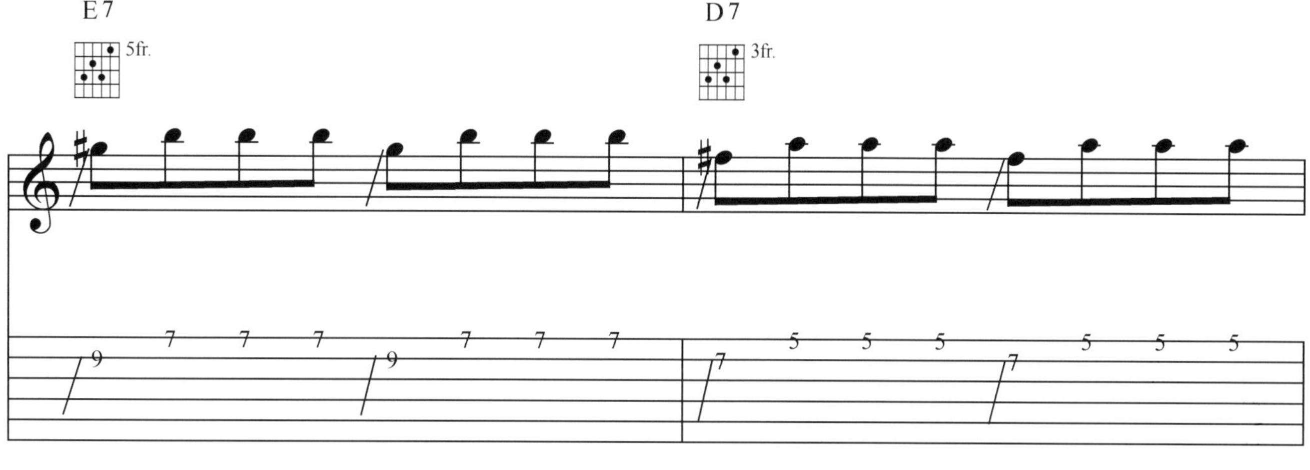
E 7
5fr.
D 7
3fr.
9
7
7
7
9
7
7
7
7
5
5
5
7
5
5
5

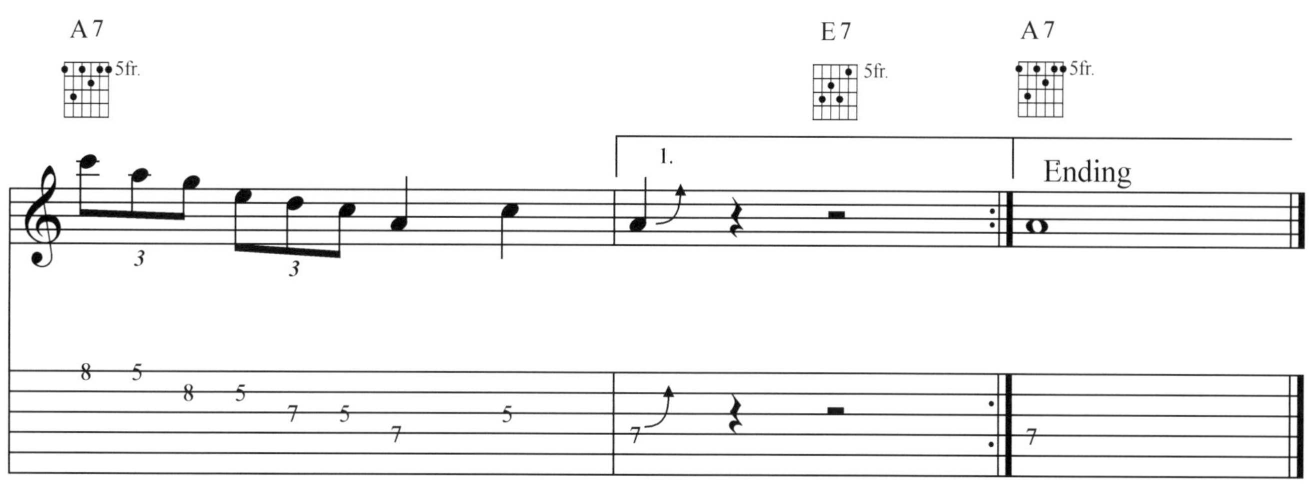
A 7
5fr.
E 7
5fr.
A 7
5fr.
1.
Ending
3
3
8
5
8
5
7
5
7
5
7
7

Amin
Pentatonic Studies

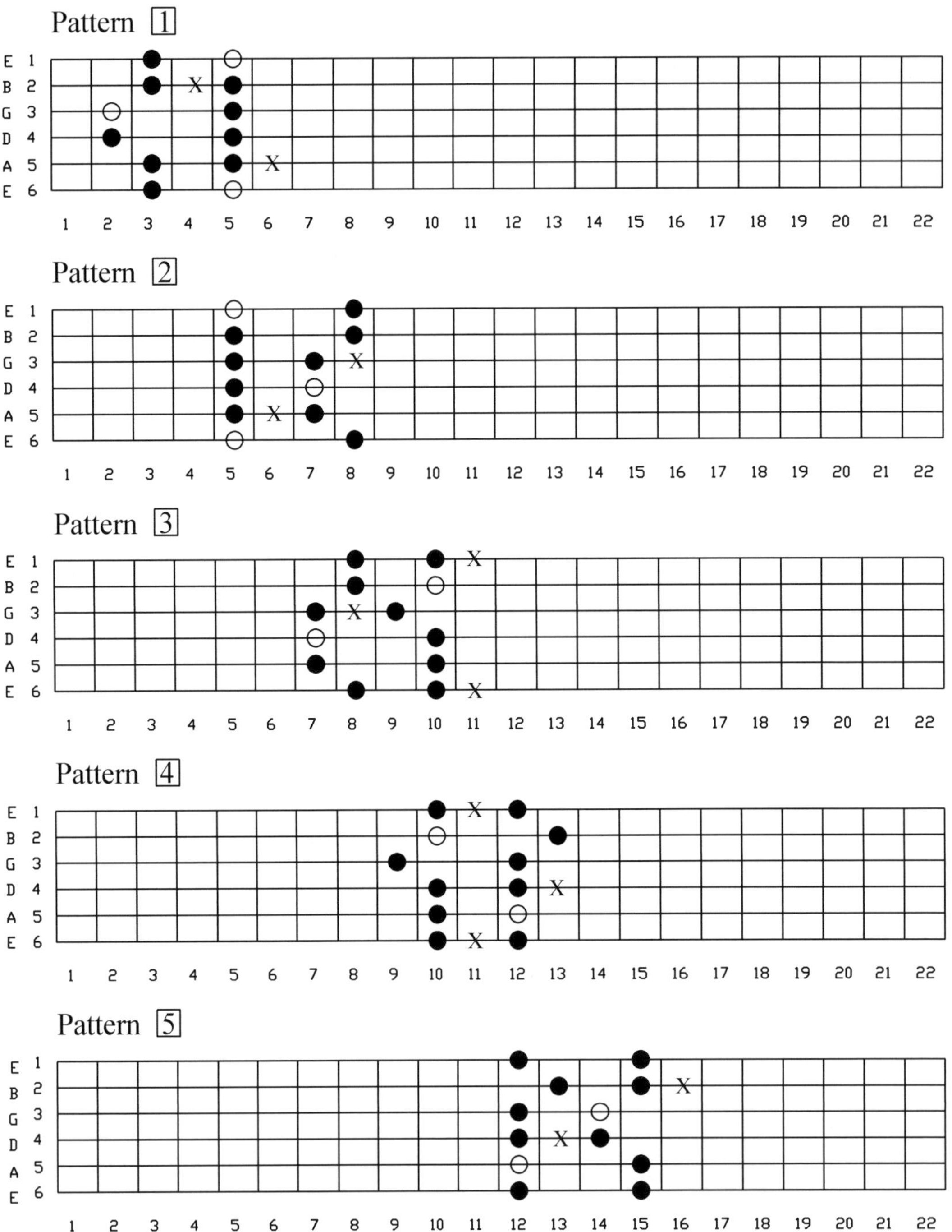

○ ROOT NOTE OF SCALE

X ADDS A FLATTED 5TH TO THE PENTATONIC SCALE TO CREATE THE BLUES SCALE

Chords

Key Center of C

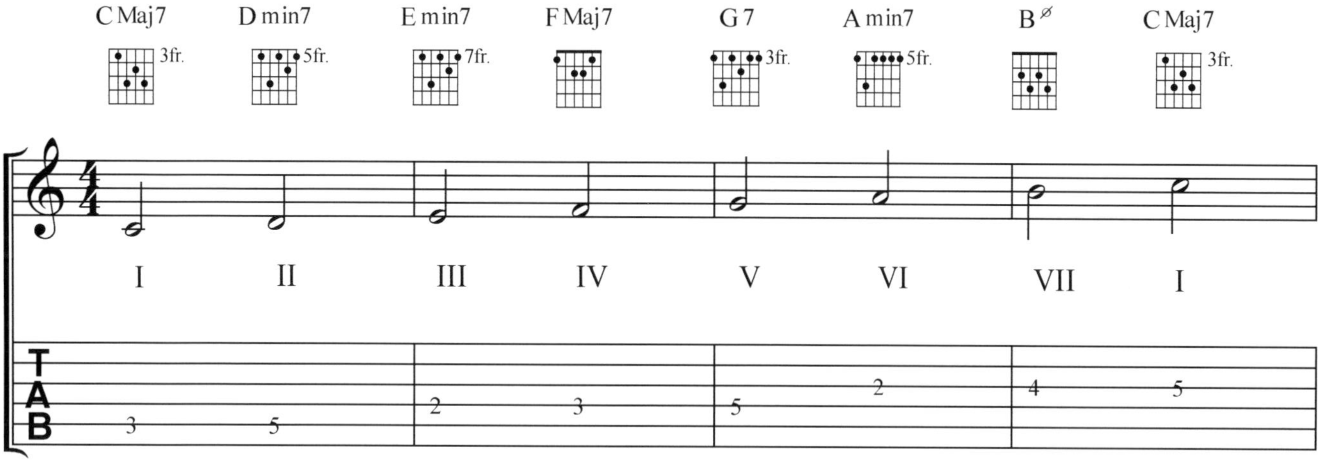

C Maj7 (3fr.) D min7 (5fr.) E min7 (7fr.) F Maj7 G 7 (3fr.) A min7 (5fr.) B ø C Maj7 (3fr.)

I II III IV V VI VII I

T A B: 3 5 | 2 3 | 5 2 | 4 5

Common Progression

C Maj7 (3fr.) A min7 (5fr.) D min7 (5fr.) G 7 (3fr.) C Maj7 (3fr.)

Track 5

1Last Time

I VI II V I

T A B: 3 3 5 | 5 3 3 | 3 3

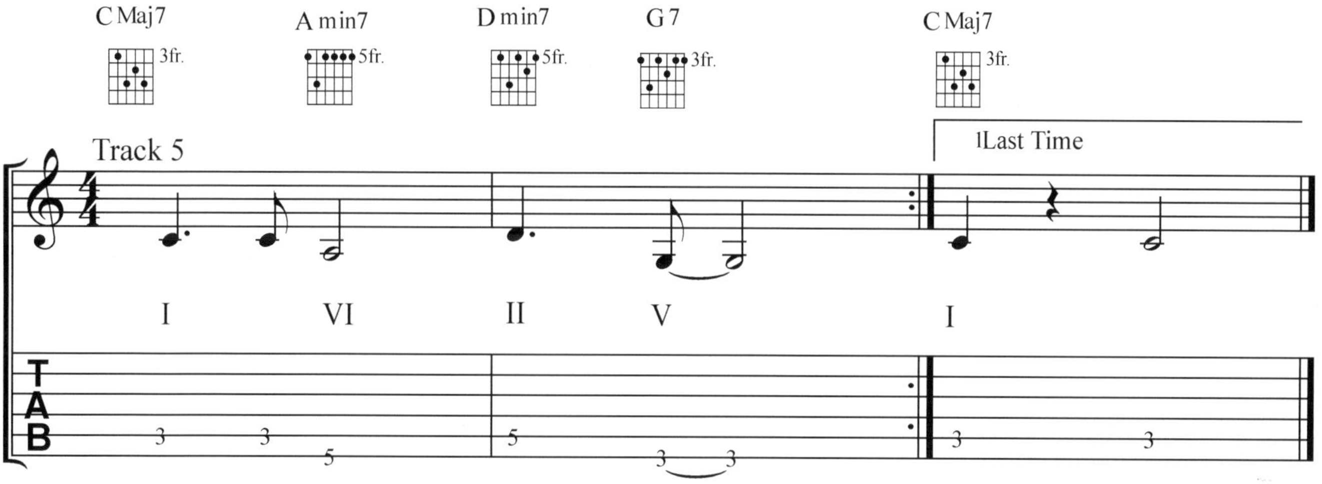

The CMaj pentatonic scale is equal to the Amin pentatonic scale. They share the same notes and are said to be enharmonic equivalents. So, use all 5 Amin pentatonic patterns to play over this CMaj progression.

Scale Studies
C = Amin Diatonic

Common Progression

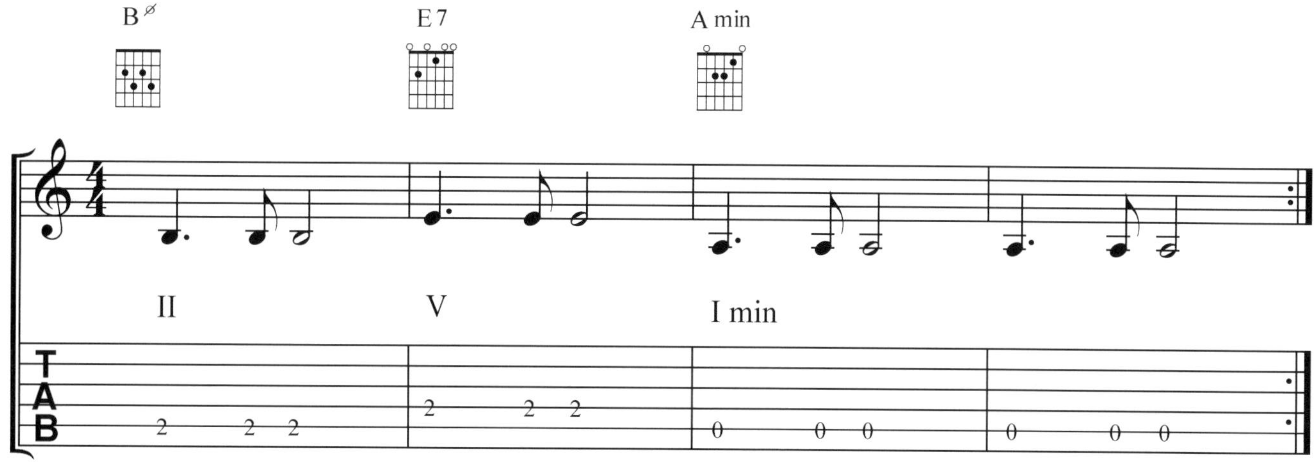

Use Amin diatonic for lead.

Diatonic Studies

C=Amin

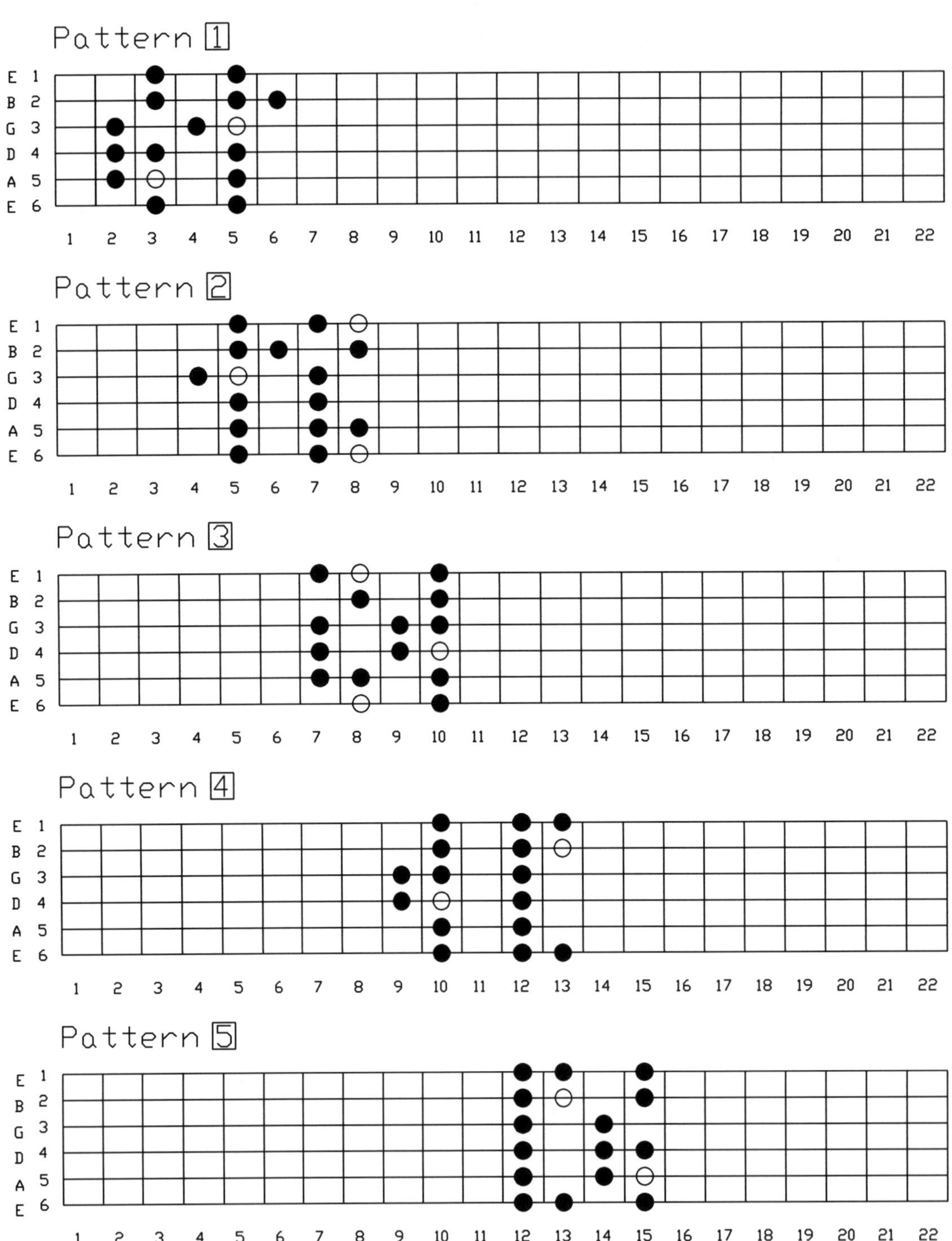

○ ROOT NOTE OF SCALE

Cycle of 5ths Progression

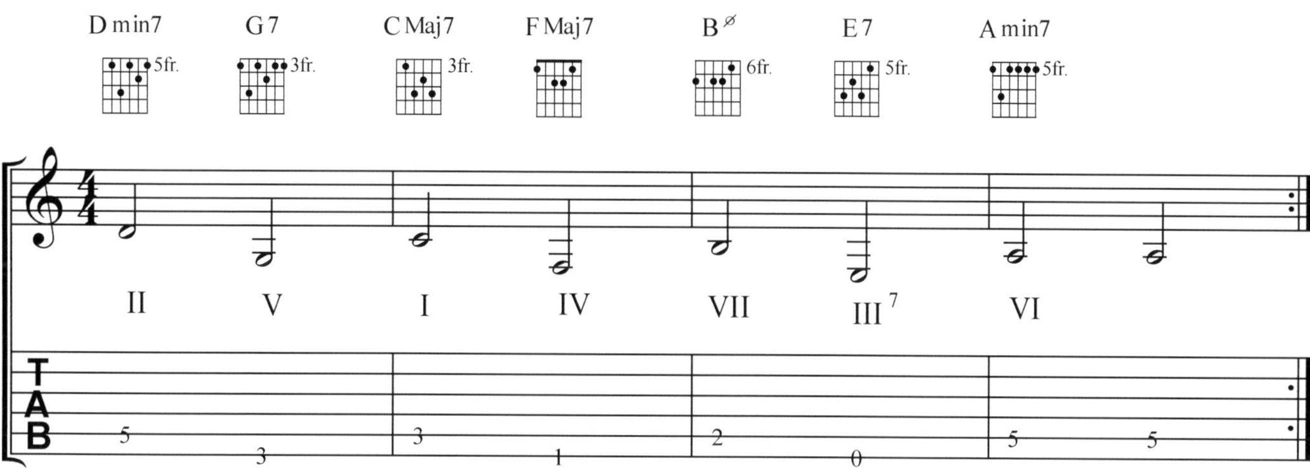

Use CMaj (Amin) diatonic scale for lead.

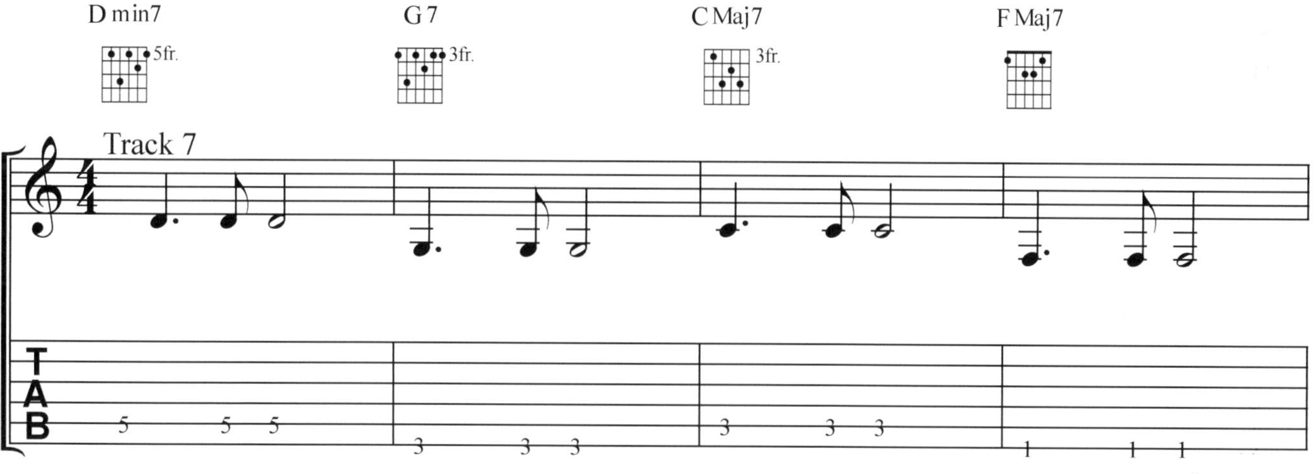

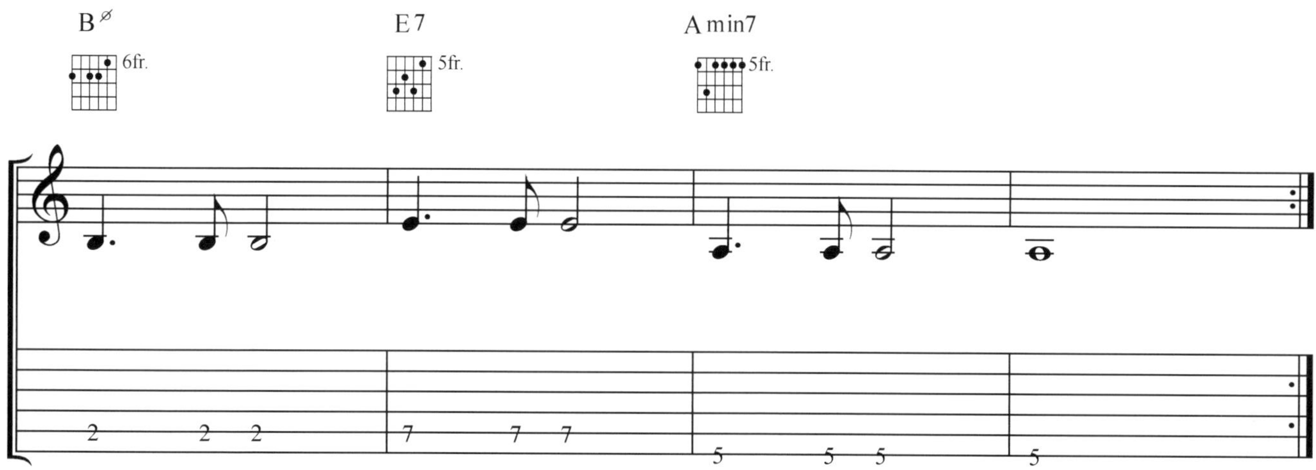

The Pentatonic Scale
Key of Gmin

Common Progressions

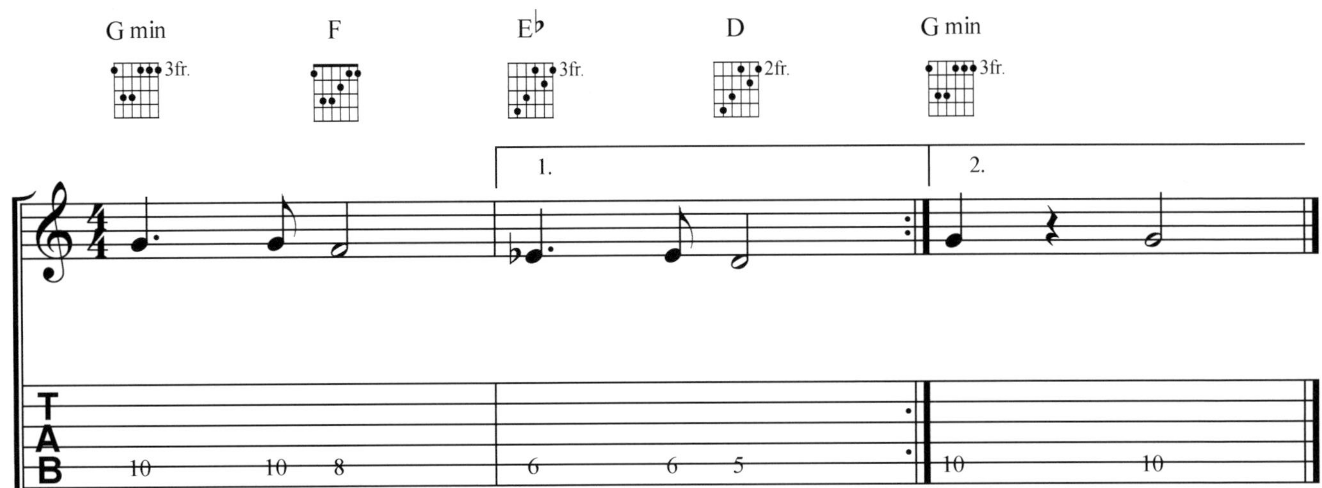

Latin Rock

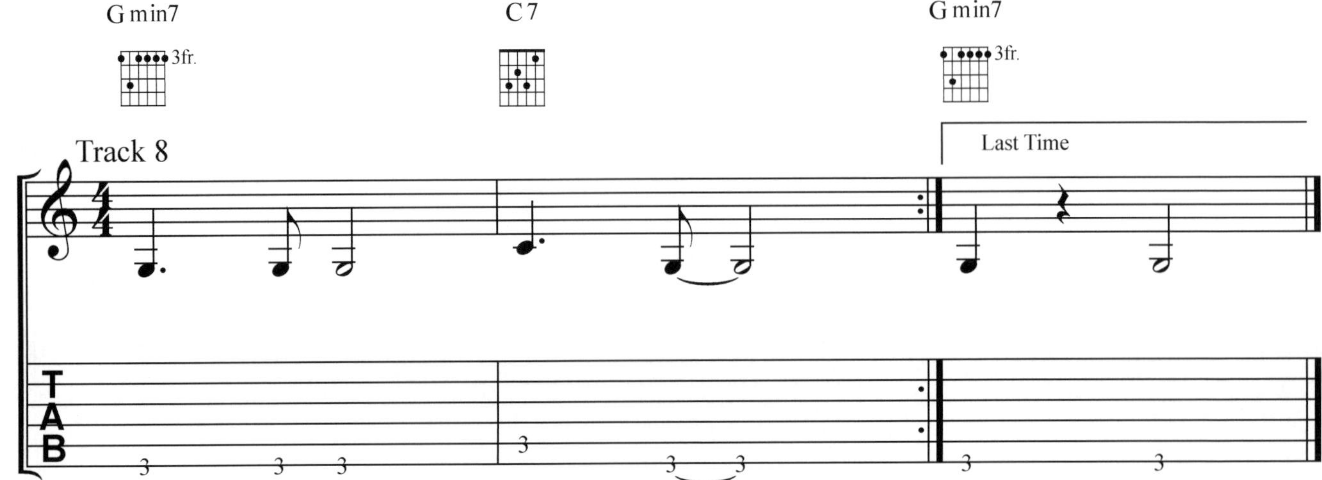

12 Bar Blues

G 7
3fr.
Track 9
T
A
B
C 7
G 7
3fr.
D 7
3fr.
C 7
G 7
3fr.
D 7
3fr.
G 7
3fr.
1.
2.

Scale Studies
Gmin Pentatonic

These are 5 different patterns at 5 positions on the fingerboard. Memorize them all and learn to shift from one to another.

G min7
10fr.
Pattern 5
13 10 13 11 12 10 12 10 13 10 13 10
10 11 10 12 10

G min7
15fr.
Pattern 1
13 15 13 15 12 15 12 15 13 15 13 15
15 15 15 15

Gmin

Pentatonic Studies

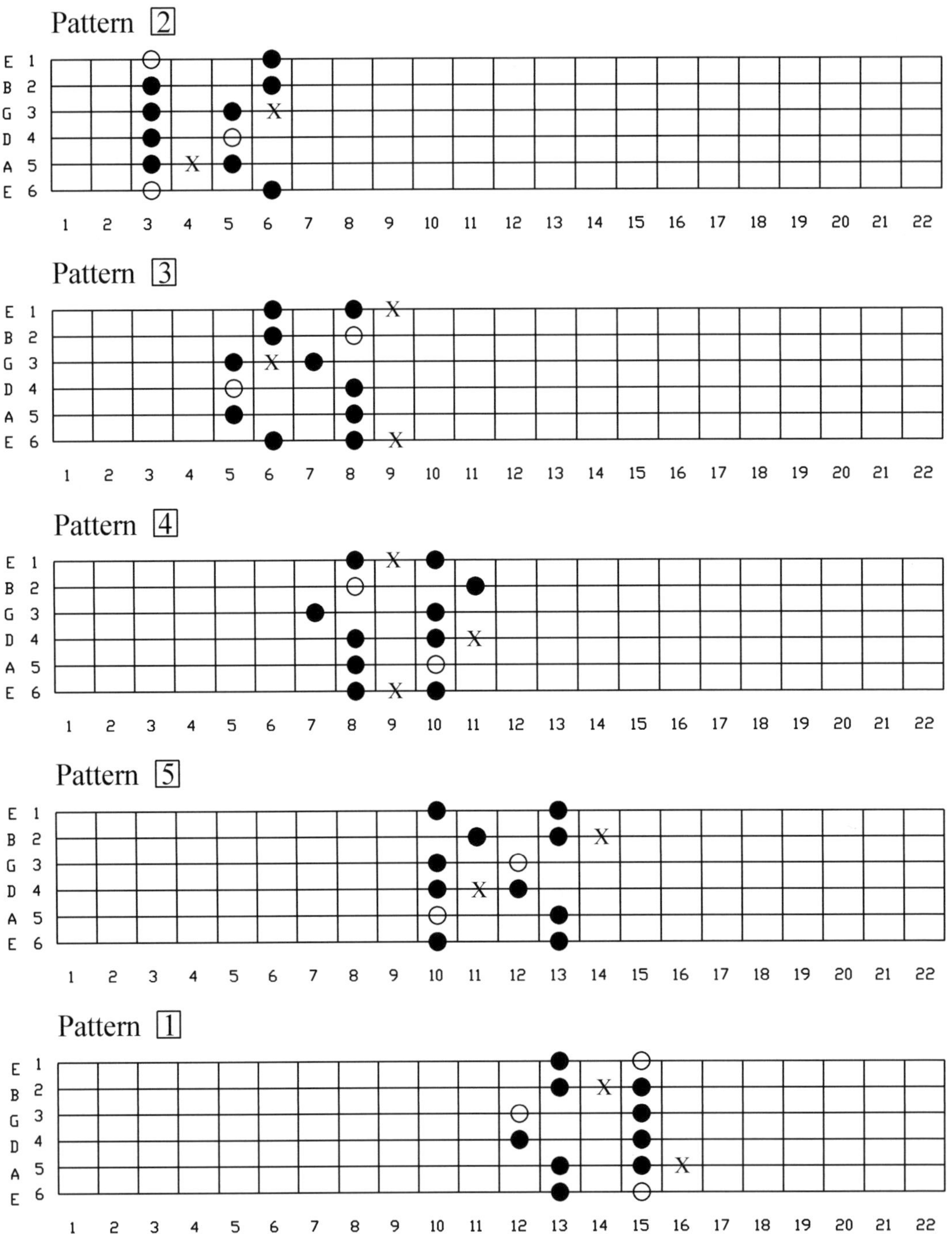

○ ROOT NOTE OF SCALE

X ADDS A FLATTED 5TH TO THE PENTATONIC SCALE TO CREATE THE BLUES SCALE

Chords

Key Center of Bb

The BbMaj pentatonic scale is equal to the Gmin pentatonic scale. They share the same notes and are said to be enharmonic equivalents. So, use all 5 Gmin pentatonic patterns to play over this BbMaj progression.

Scale Studies
Bb = Gmin Diatonic

Common Progression

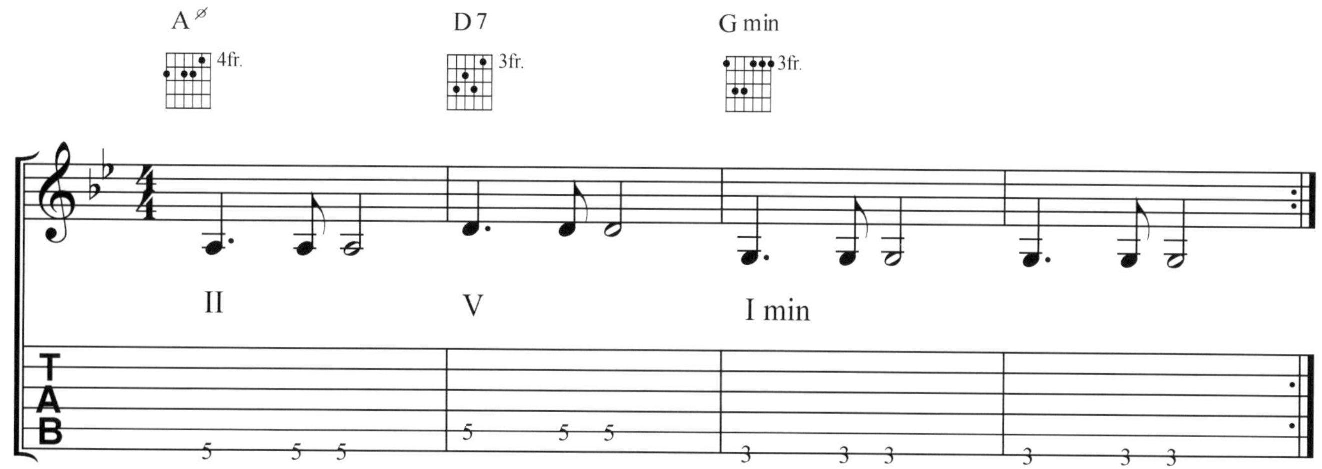

Use Gmin diatonic for lead.

Diatonic Studies

Bb=Gmin

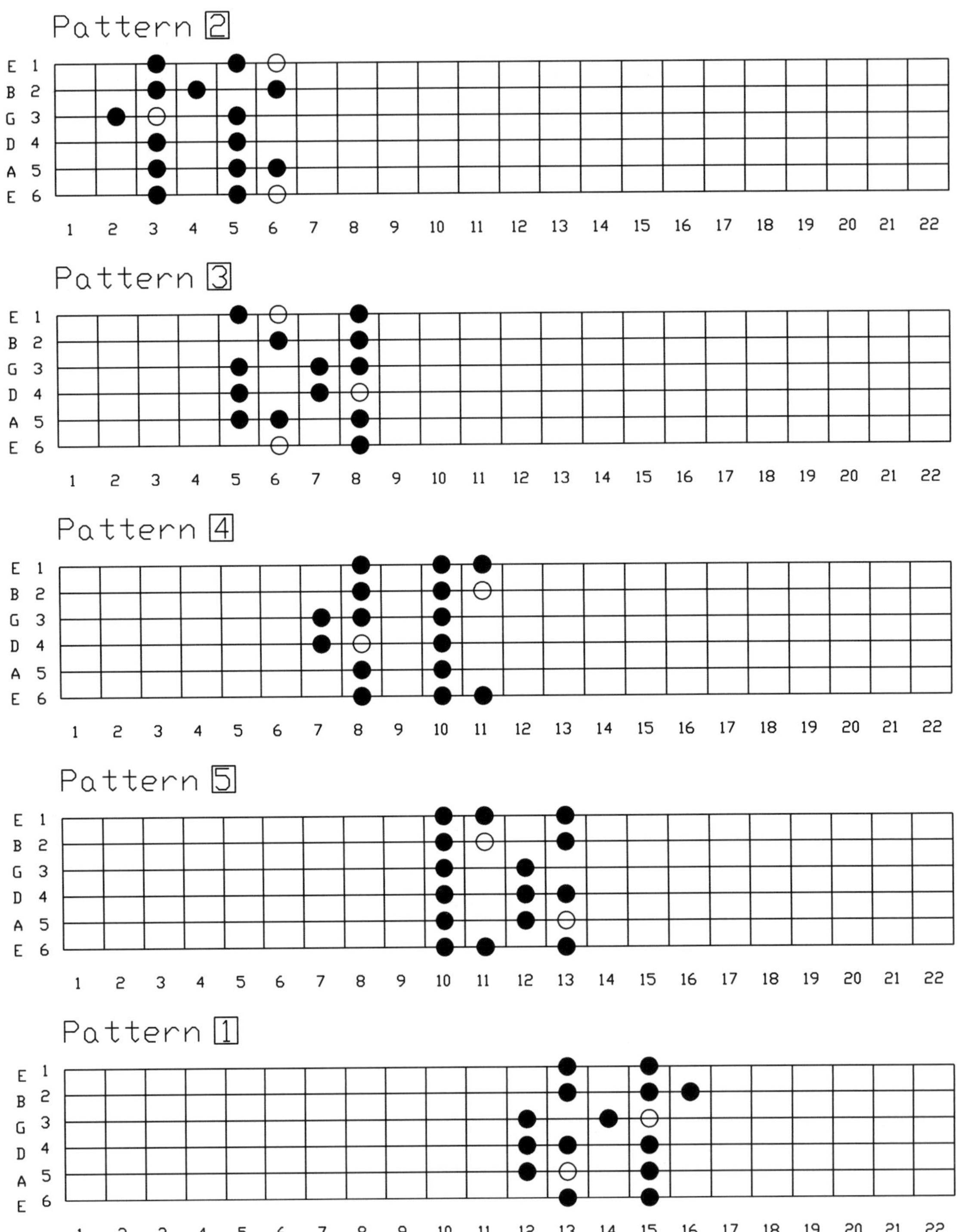

○ ROOT NOTE OF SCALE

Cycle of 5ths Progression

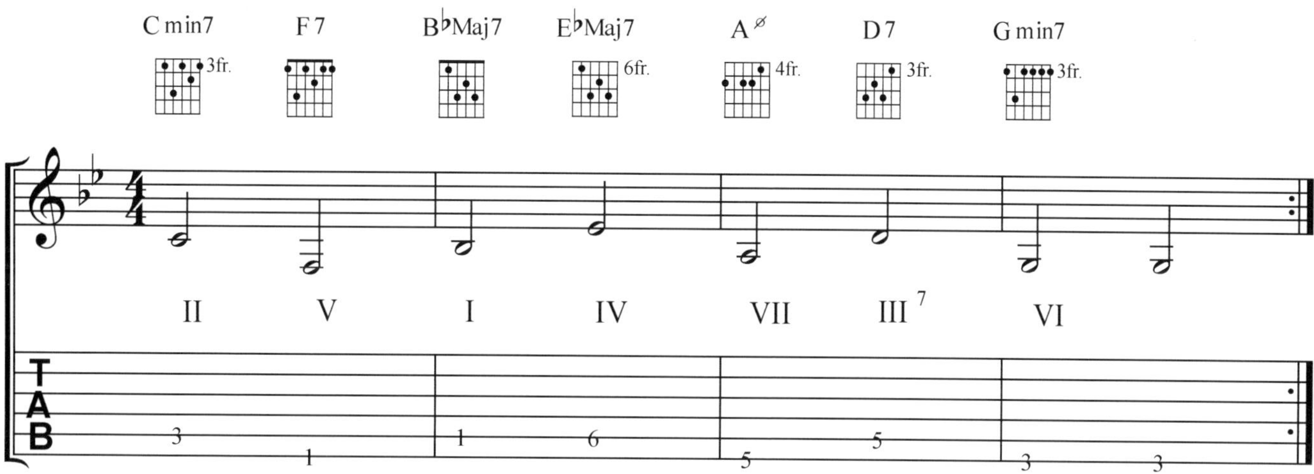

Use BbMaj (Gmin) diatonic scale for lead.

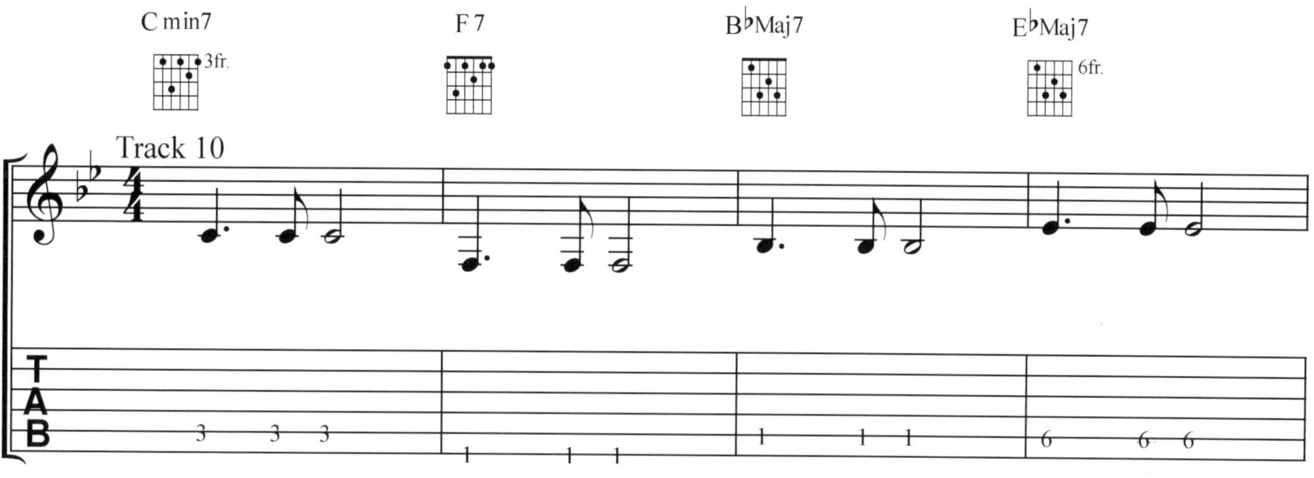

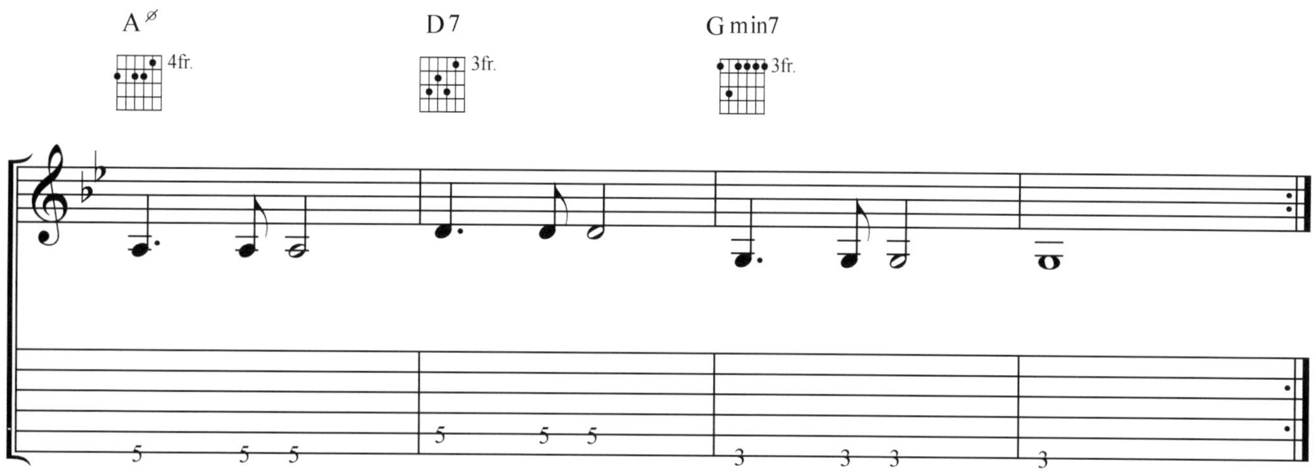

The Pentatonic Scale
Key of Bbmin

Common Progressions

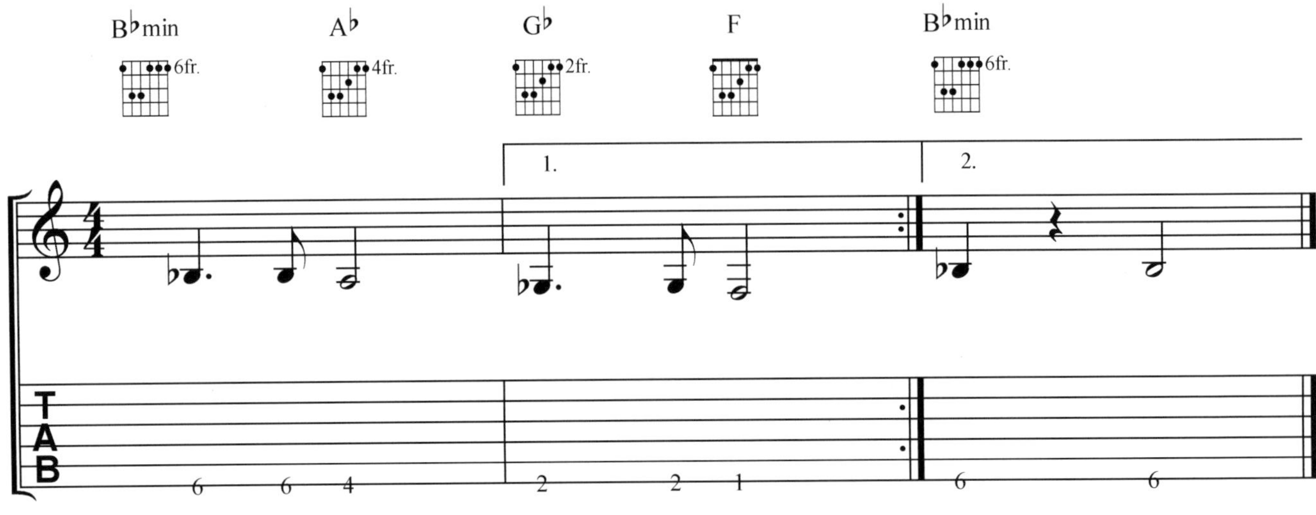

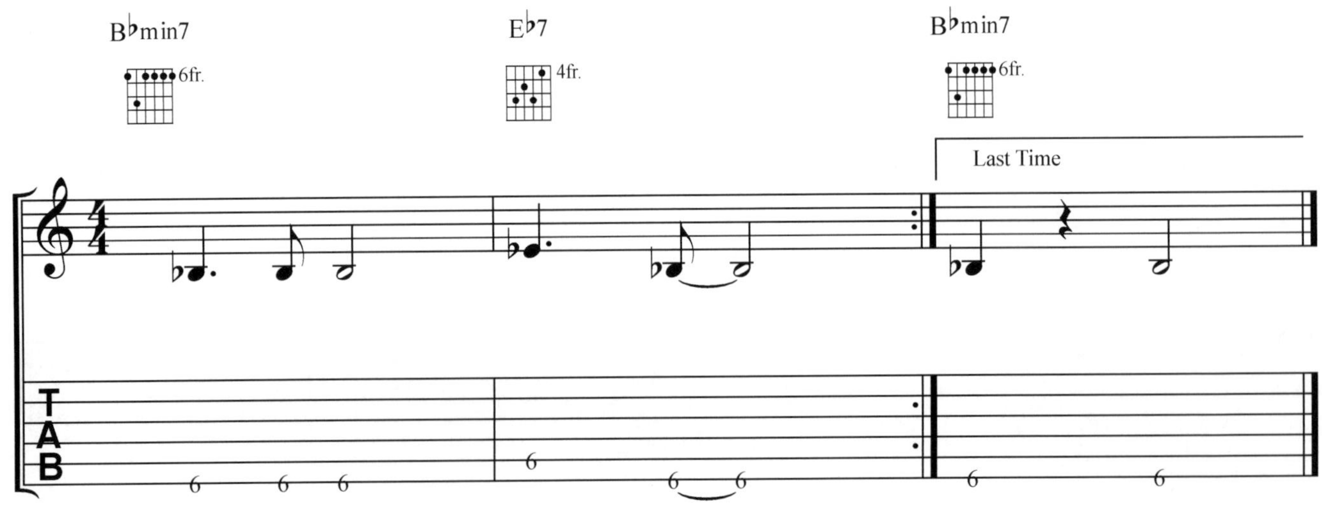

12 Bar Blues

B♭7
6fr.
Track 12
E♭7
4fr.
B♭7
6fr.
F 7
6fr.
E♭7
4fr.
B♭7
6fr.
F 7
6fr.
B♭7
6fr.
1.
2.

Scale Studies
Bbmin Pentatonic

These are 5 different patterns at 5 positions on the fingerboard. Memorize them all and learn to shift from one to another.

Bbmin7
8fr.
Pattern 3
11 9 11 9 10 8 11 8
11 8 11 9
9 9 10 8

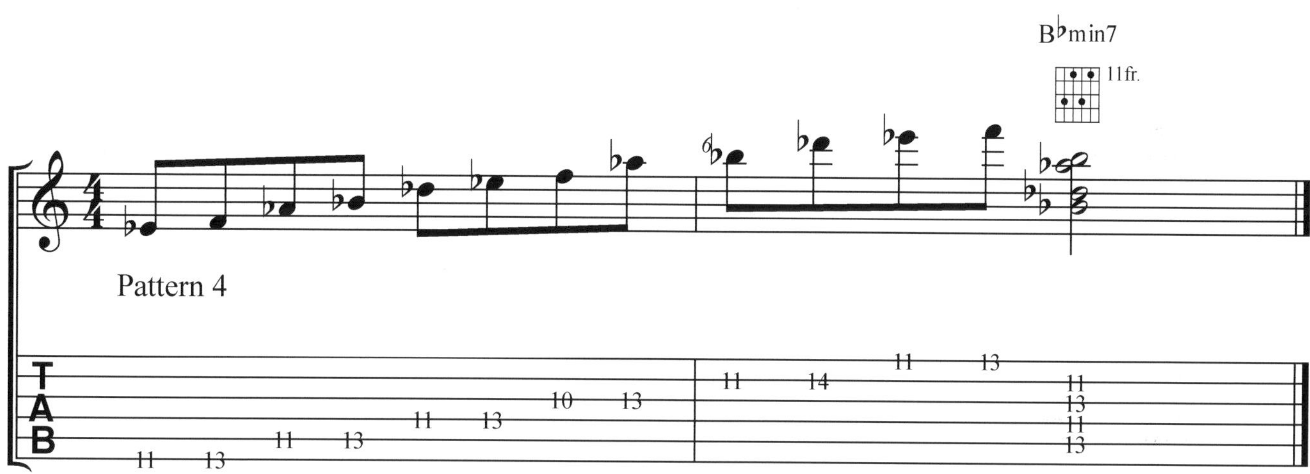
Bbmin7
11fr.
Pattern 4
11 13 11 13 11 13 10 13
11 14 11 13
11 13 11 13

Bbmin
Pentatonic Studies

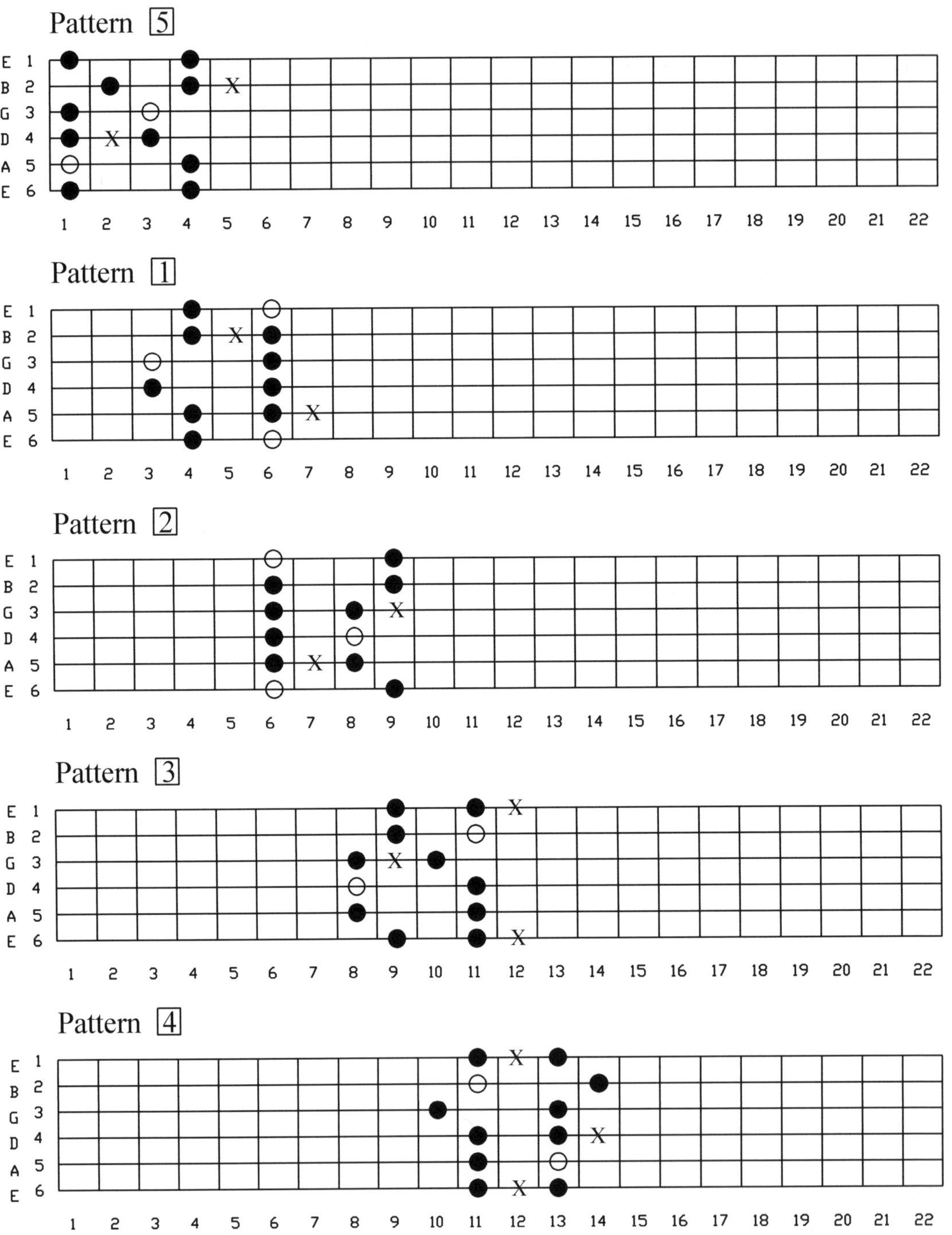

○ ROOT NOTE OF SCALE

X ADDS A FLATTED 5TH TO THE PENTATONIC SCALE TO CREATE THE BLUES SCALE

Chords

Key Center of Db

The DbMaj pentatonic scale is equal to the Bbmin pentatonic scale. They share the same notes and are said to be enharmonic equivalents. So, use all 5 Bbmin pentatonic patterns to play over this DbMaj progression.

Scale Studies
Db = Bbmin Diatonic

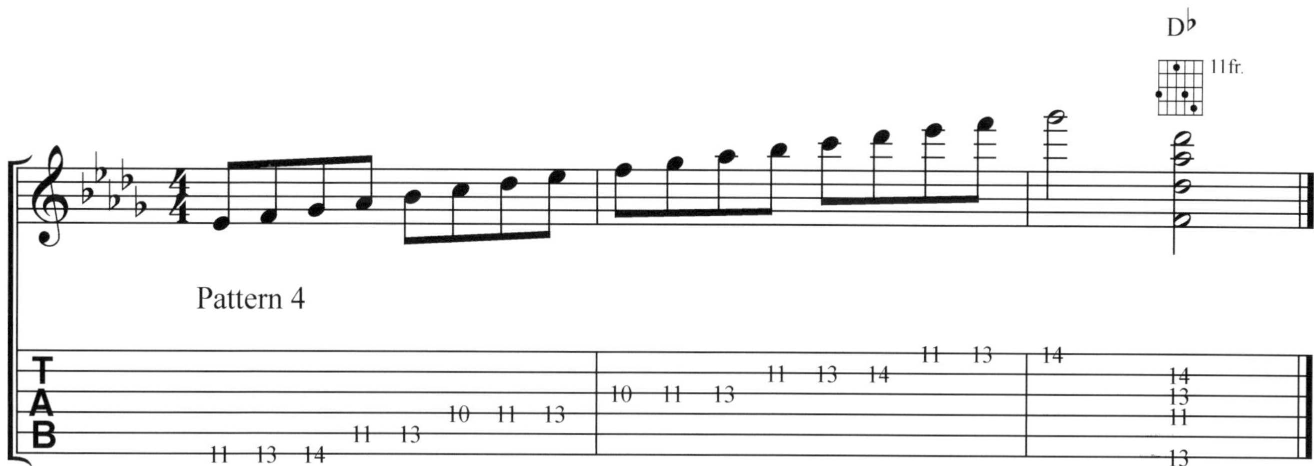

Common Progression

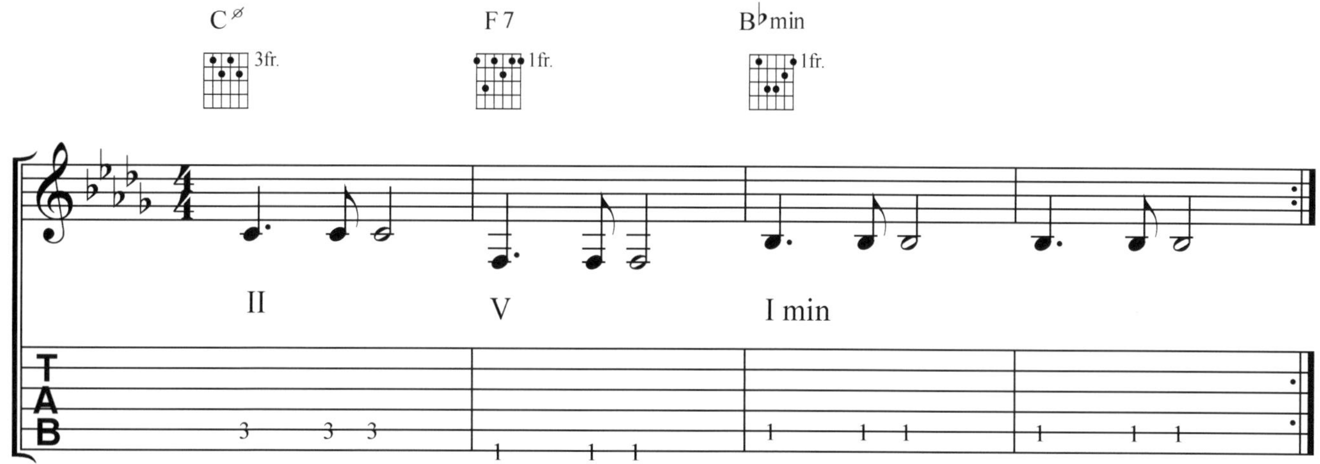

Use Bbmin diatonic for lead.

Diatonic Studies

Db=Bbmin

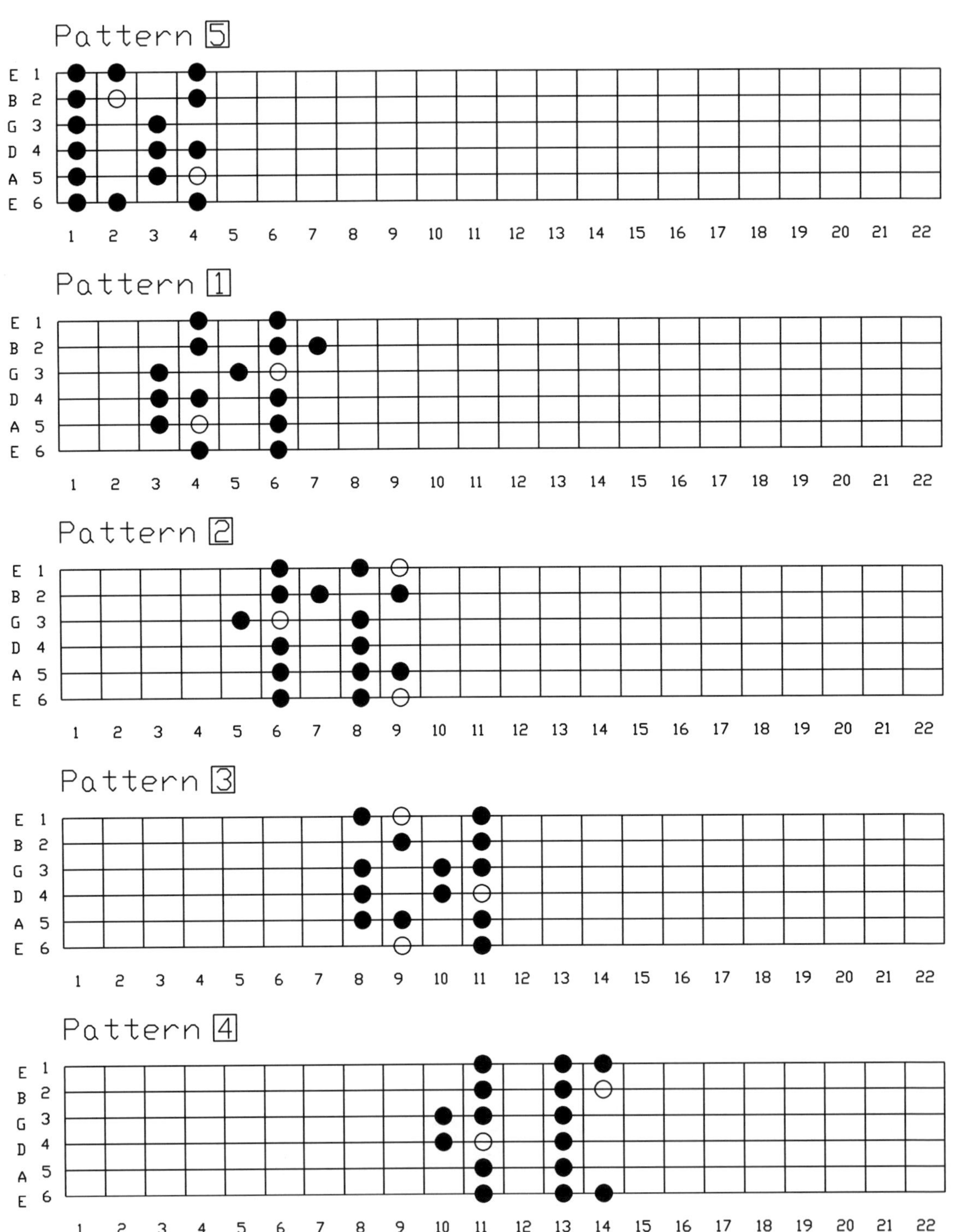

○ ROOT NOTE OF SCALE

Cycle of 5ths Progression

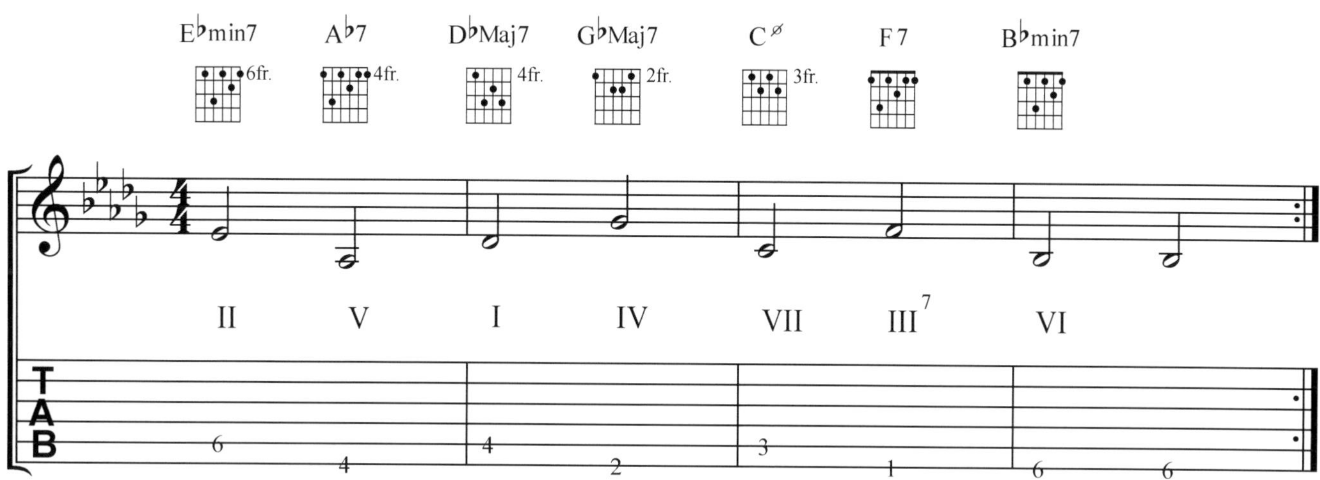

Use DbMaj (Bbmin) diatonic scale for lead.

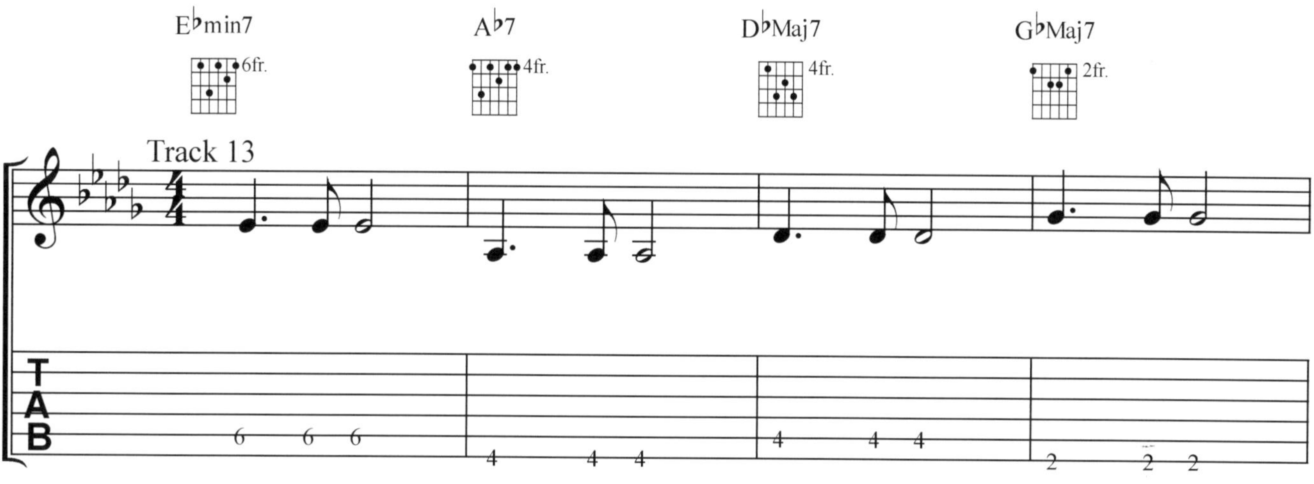

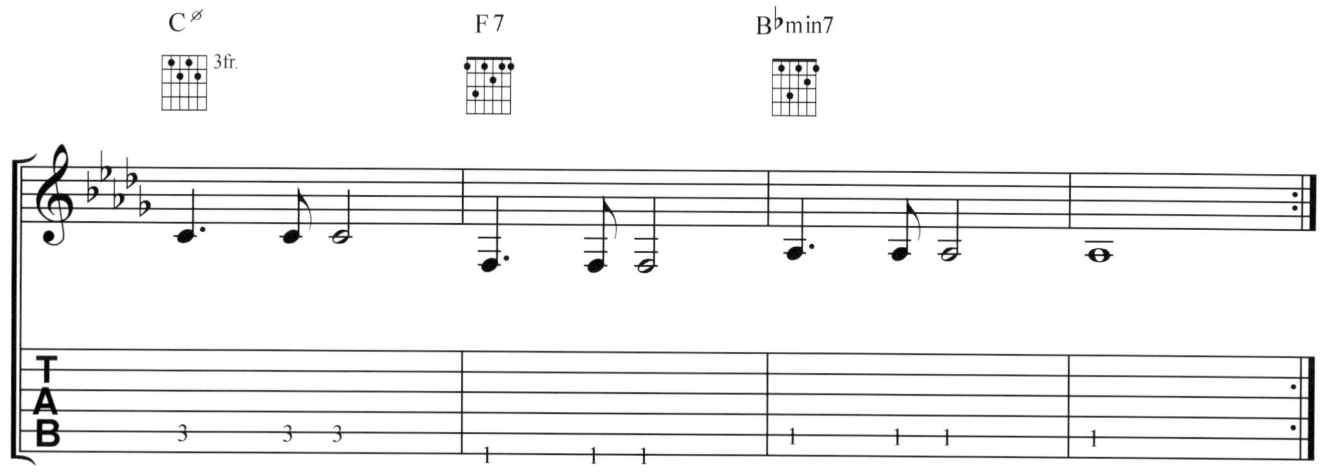

The Pentatonic Scale
Key of Cmin

Common Progressions

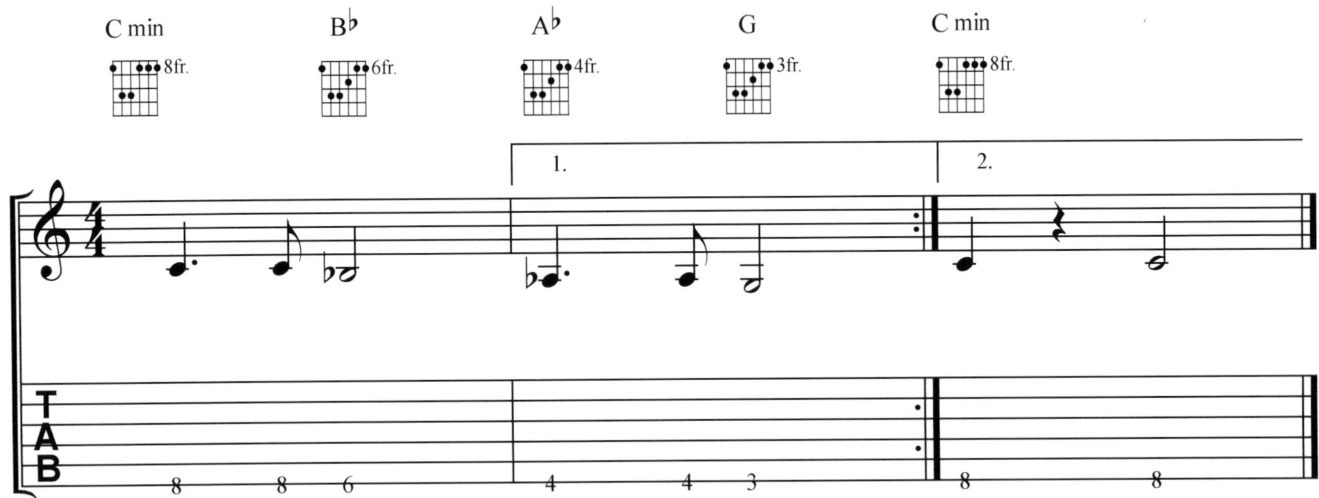

Latin Rock

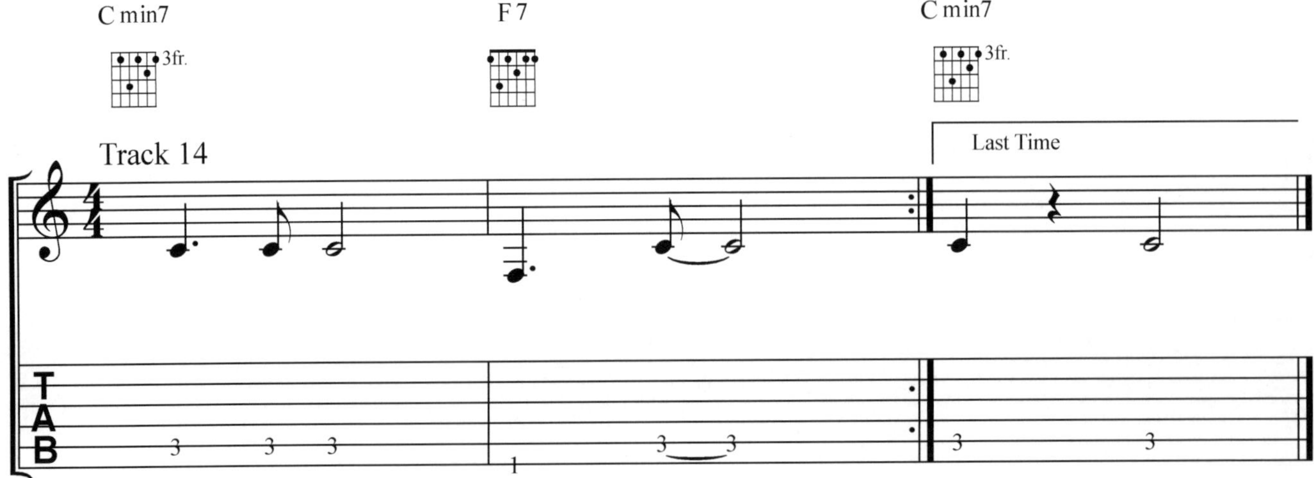

12 Bar Blues

C 7
8fr.
Track 15
F 7
6fr.
C 7
8fr.
G 7
8fr.
F 7
6fr.
C 7
8fr.
G 7
8fr.
C 7
8fr.
1.
2.

Scale Studies
Cmin Pentatonic

These are 5 different patterns at 5 positions on the fingerboard. Memorize them all and learn to shift from one to another.

C min7
10fr.
Pattern 3
T
A
B
13 11
13 11
12 10
13 10
13 10
13 11
11
11
12
10

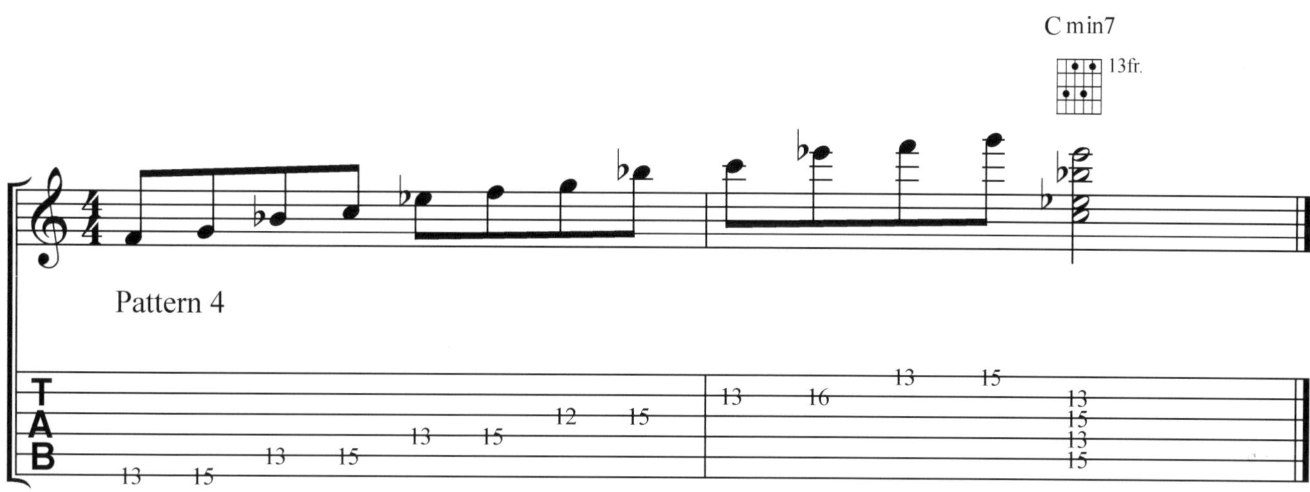
C min7
13fr.
Pattern 4
T
A
B
13 15
13 15
13 15
12 15
13 16
13 15
13
15
13
15

Cmin
Pentatonic Studies

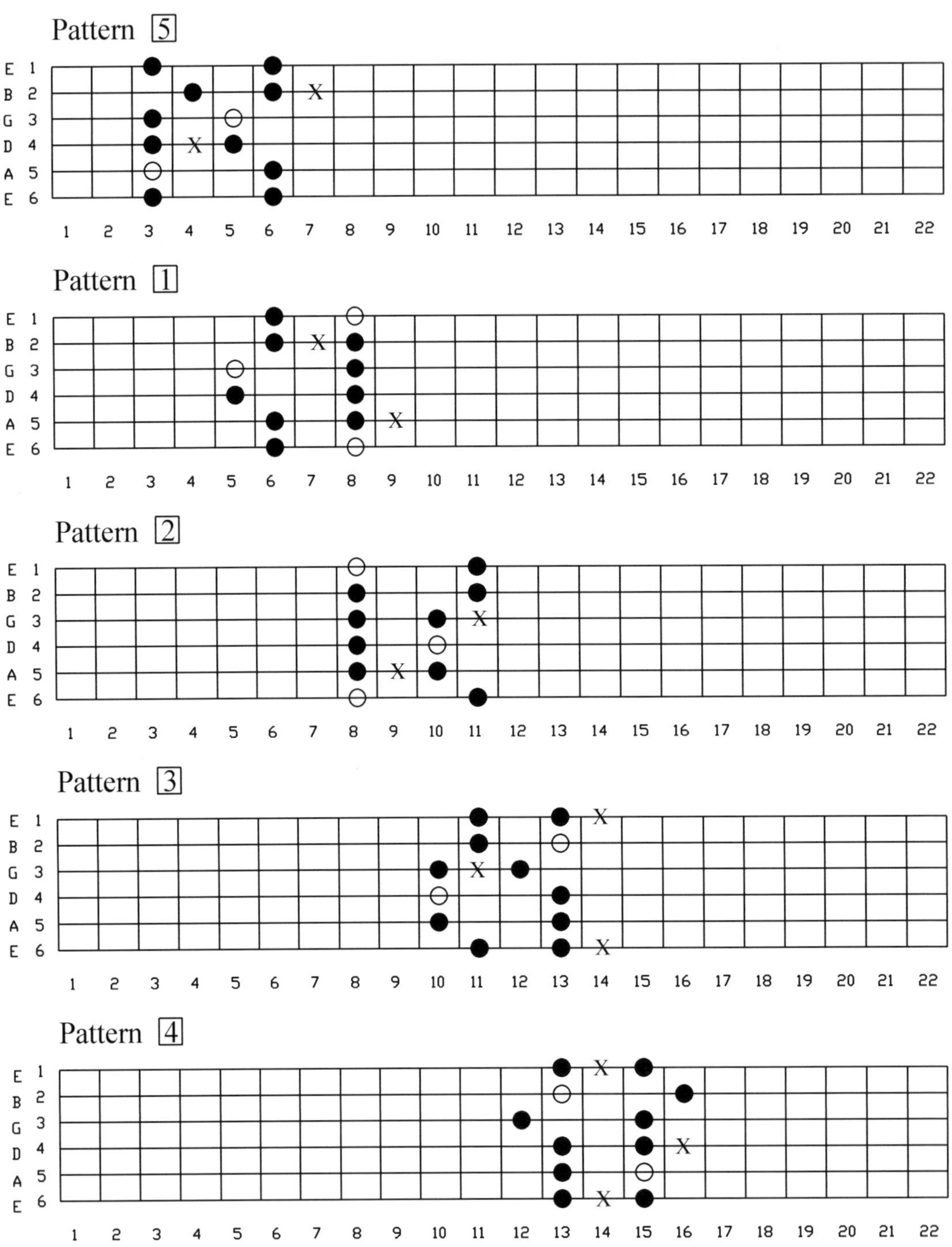

○ ROOT NOTE OF SCALE

X ADDS A FLATTED 5TH TO THE PENTATONIC SCALE TO CREATE THE BLUES SCALE

Chords

Key Center of Eb

The EbMaj pentatonic scale is equal to the Cmin pentatonic scale. They share the same notes and are said to be enharmonic equivalents. So, use all 5 Cmin pentatonic patterns to play over this EbMaj progression.

Scale Studies
Eb = Cmin Diatonic

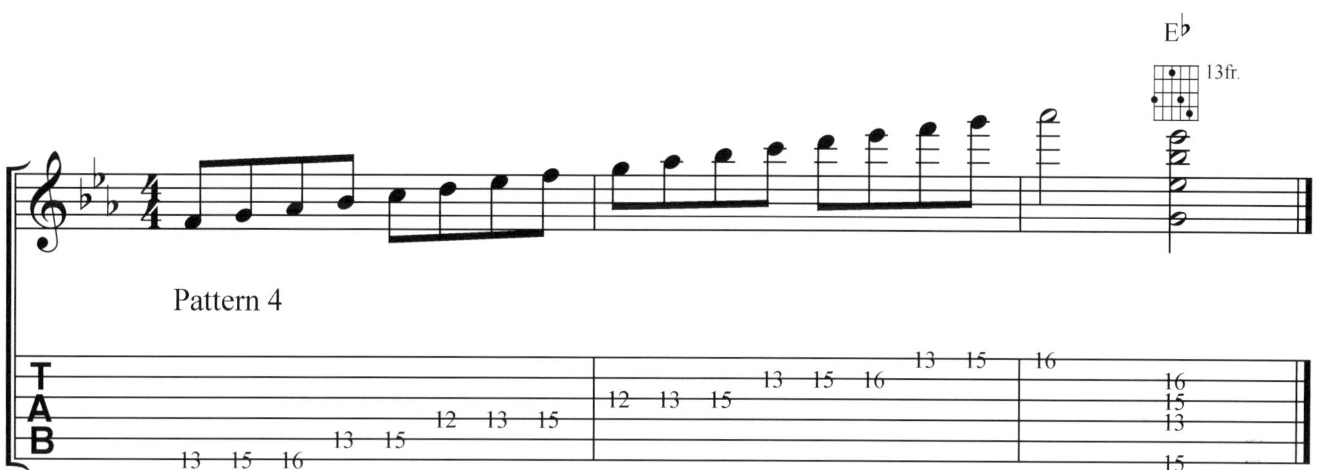

Common Progression

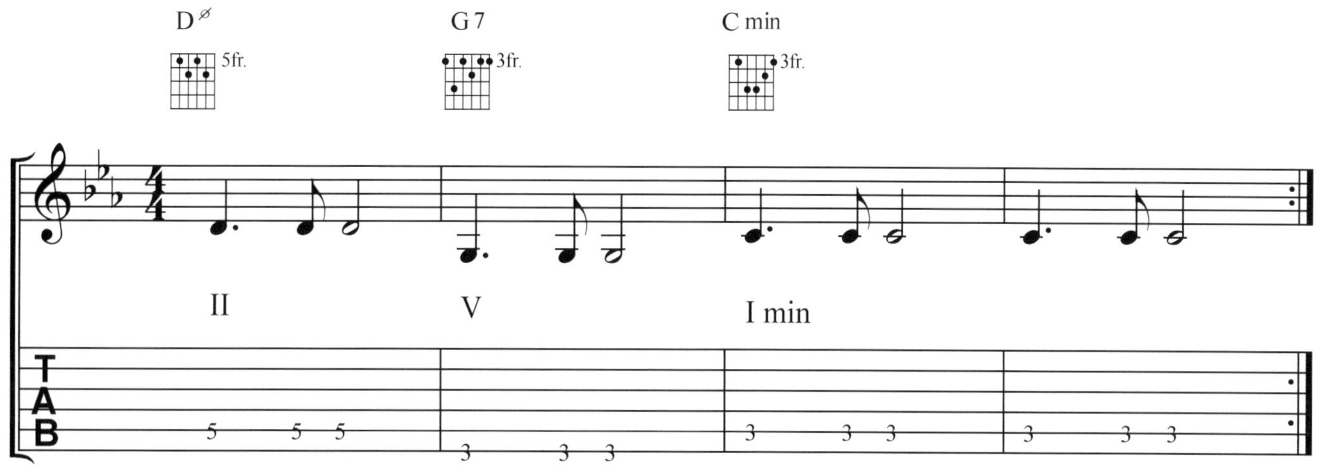

Use Cmin diatonic for lead.

Diatonic Studies

Eb=Cmin

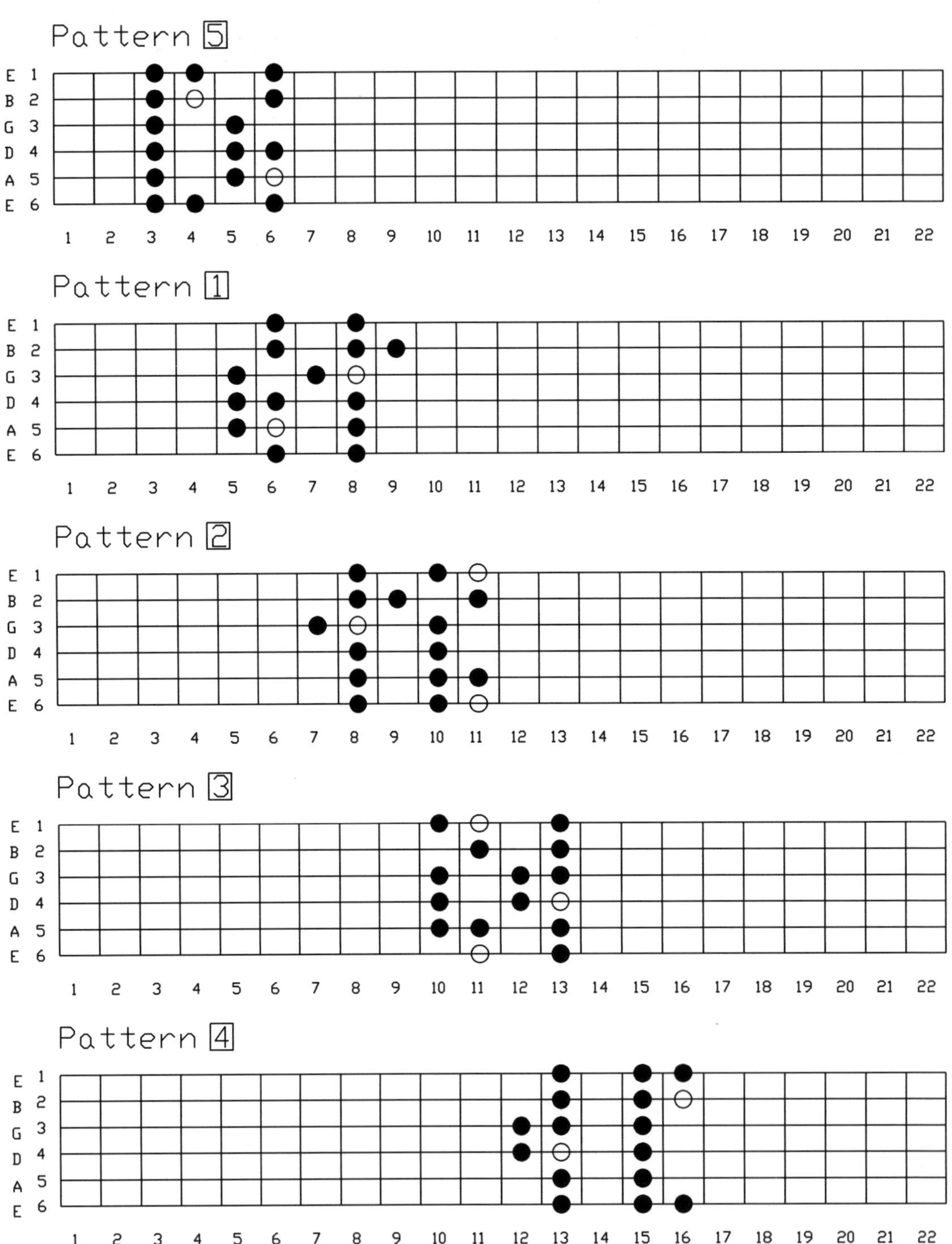

○ ROOT NOTE OF SCALE

Cycle of 5ths Progression

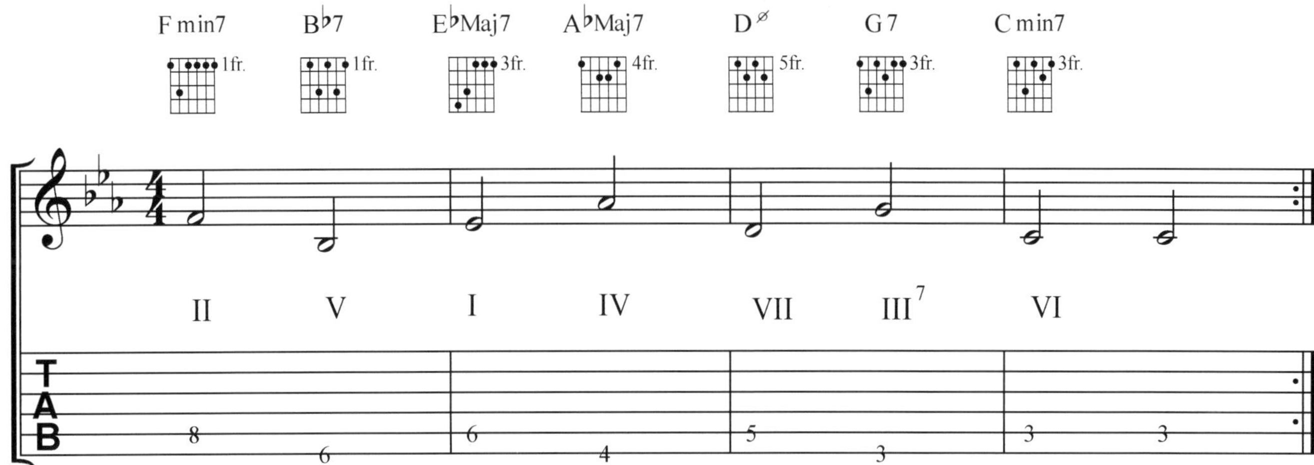

Use EbMaj (Cmin) diatonic scale for lead.

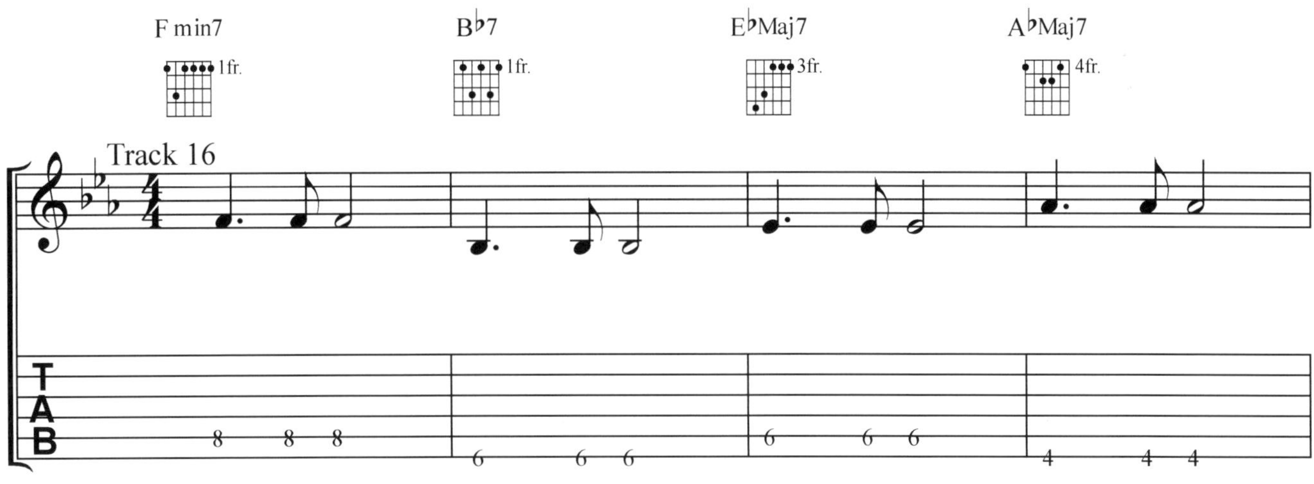

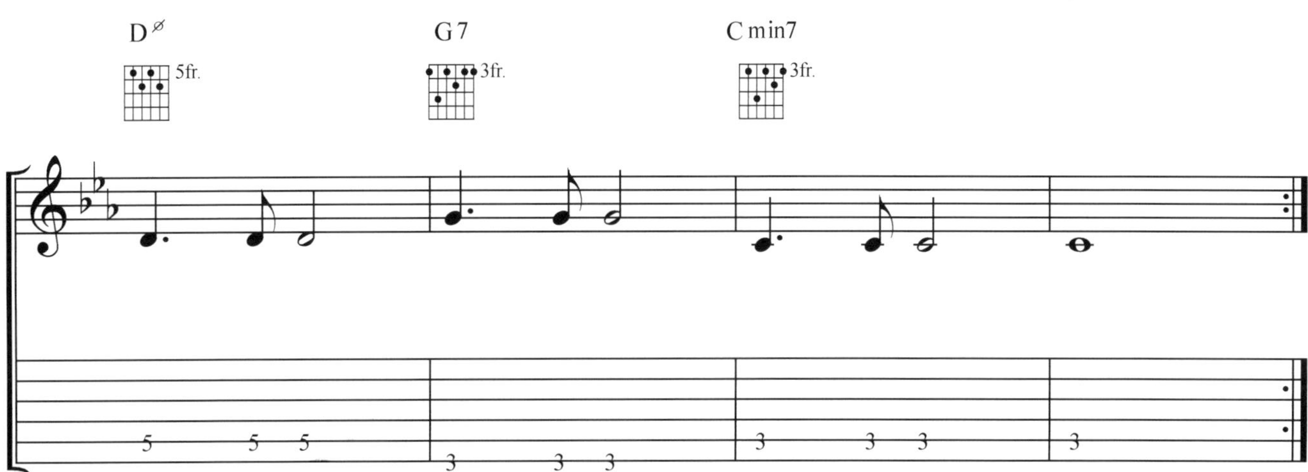

The Pentatonic Scale
Key of Emin

Common Progressions

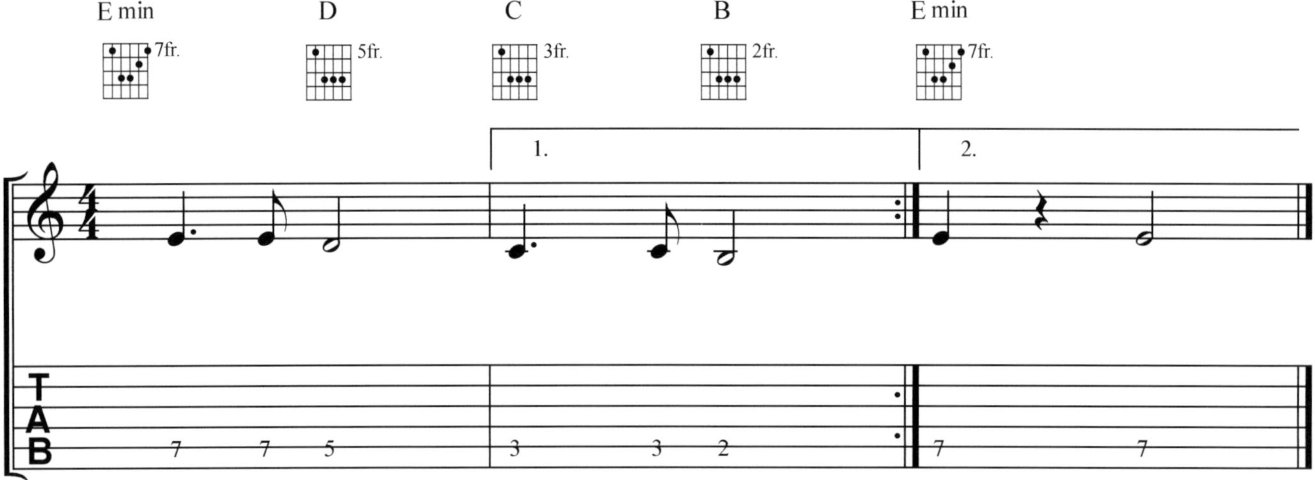

Latin Rock

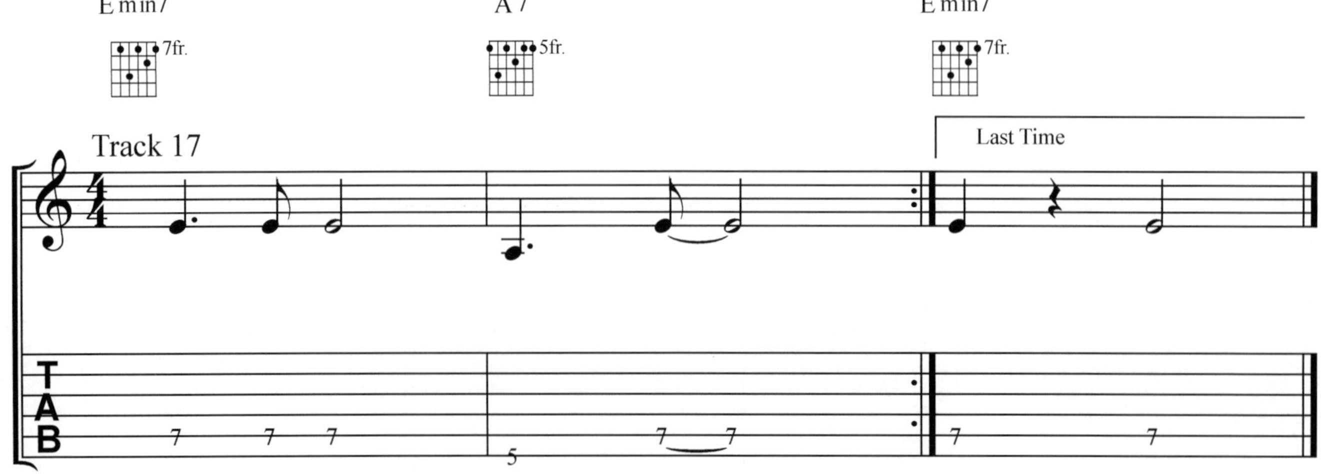

12 Bar Blues

E7
5fr.
Track 18
A7
5fr.
E7
5fr.
B7
7fr.
A7
5fr.
E7
5fr.
B7
7fr.
E7
5fr.
1.
2.

Scale Studies
Emin Pentatonic

These are 5 different patterns at 5 positions on the fingerboard. Memorize them all and learn to shift from one to another.

E min7
12fr.
Pattern 1
TAB
12 10 12 10 12 9 12 9 12 10 12 10
12
12
12
12

E min7
12fr.
Pattern 2
TAB
12 15 12 14 12 14 12 14 12 15 12 15
12
12
12
12
14
12

Emin
Pentatonic Studies

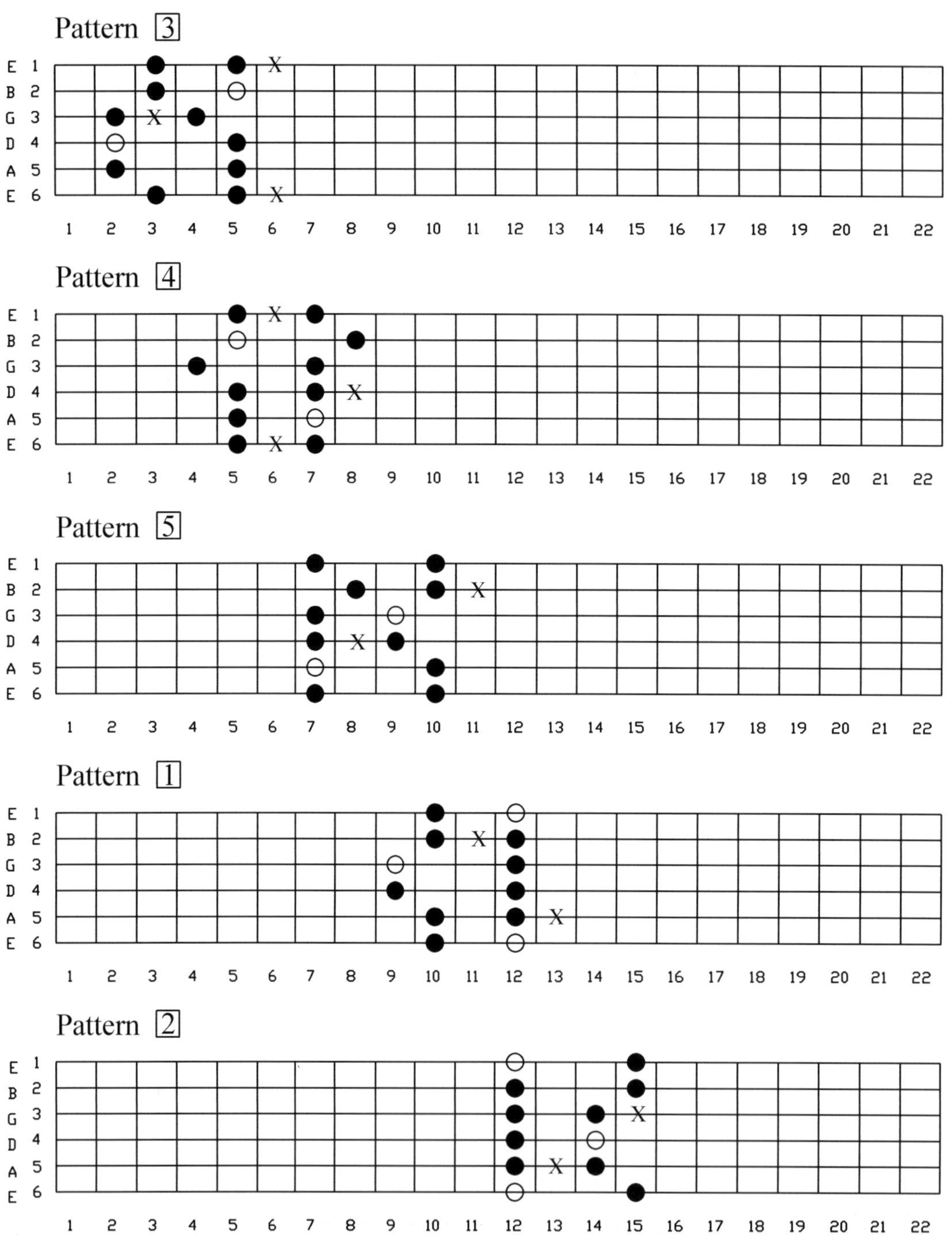

○ ROOT NOTE OF SCALE

X ADDS A FLATTED 5TH TO THE PENTATONIC SCALE TO CREATE THE BLUES SCALE

Chords

Key Center of G

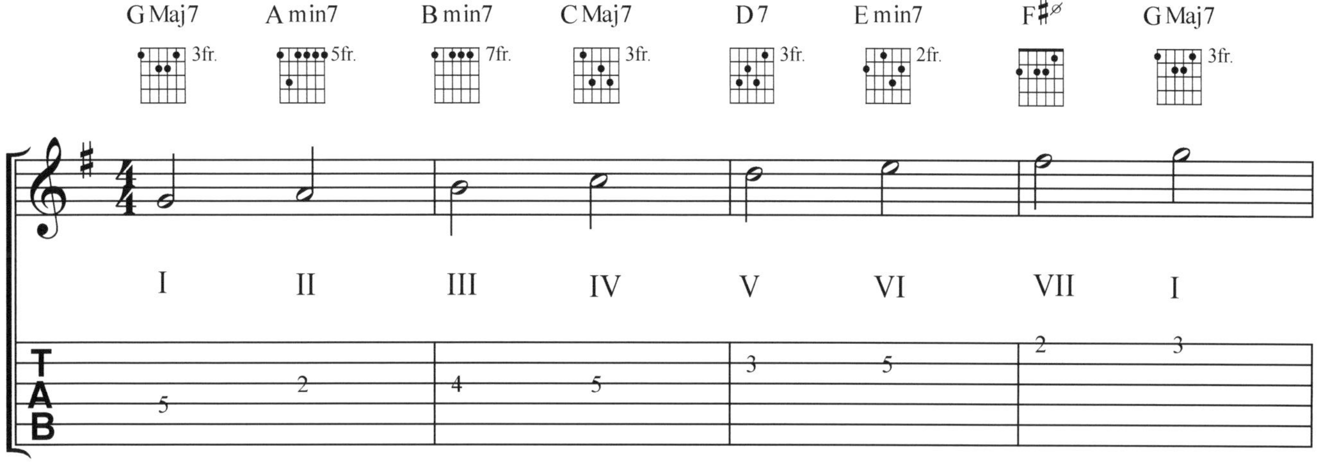

Common Progression

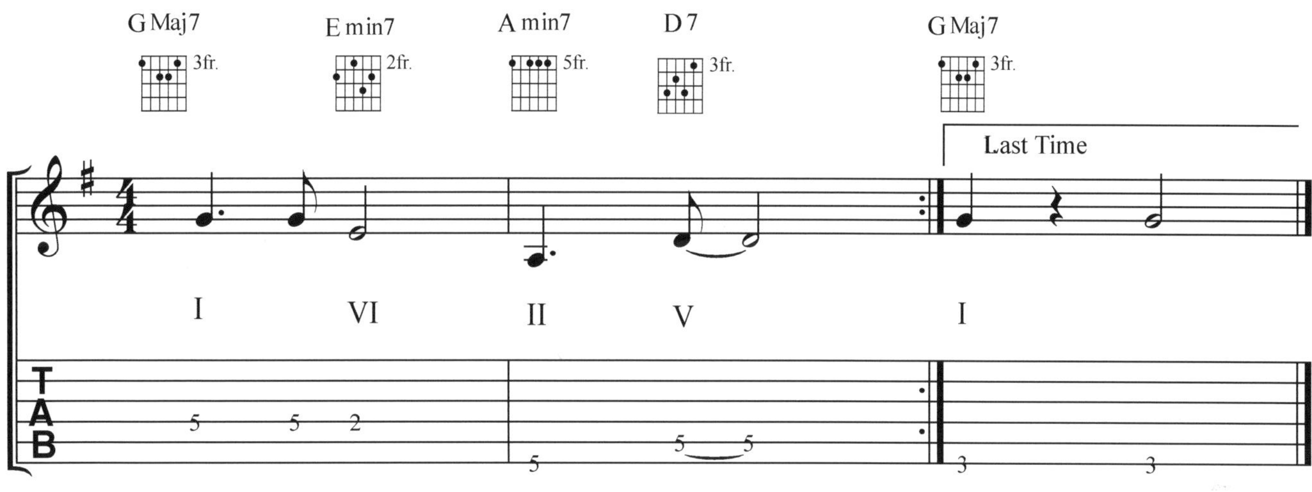

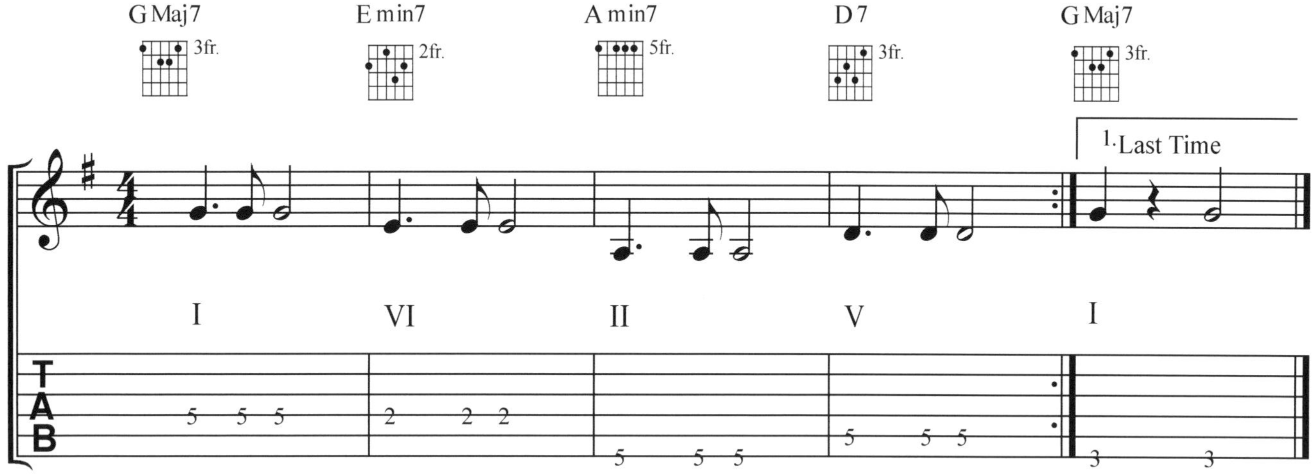

The GMaj pentatonic scale is equal to the Emin pentatonic scale. They share the same notes and are said to be enharmonic equivalents. So, use all 5 Emin pentatonic patterns to play over this GMaj progression.

Scale Studies
G = Emin Diatonic

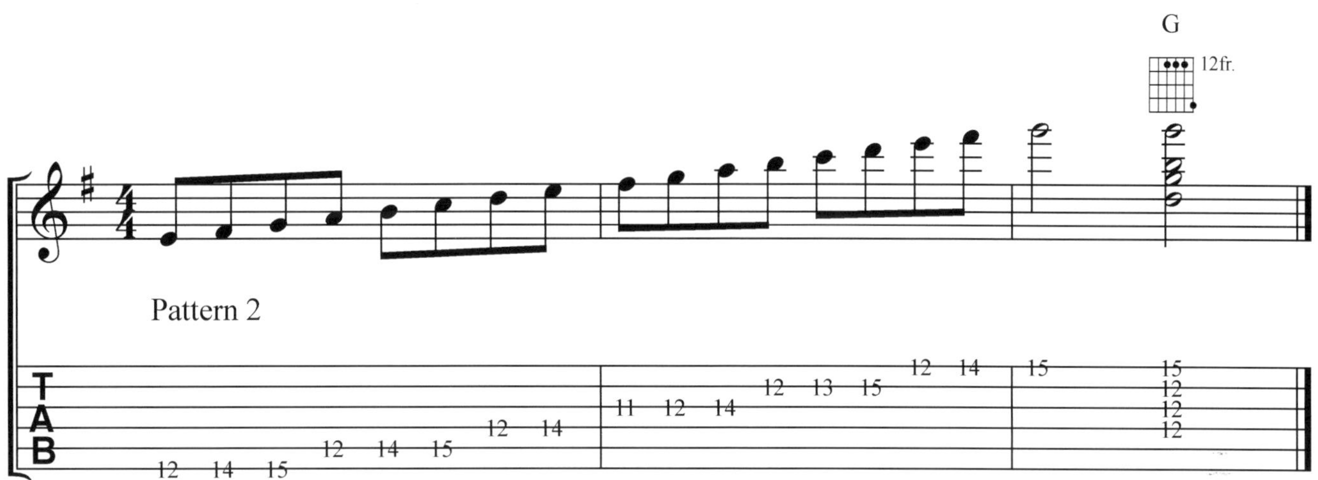

Common Progression

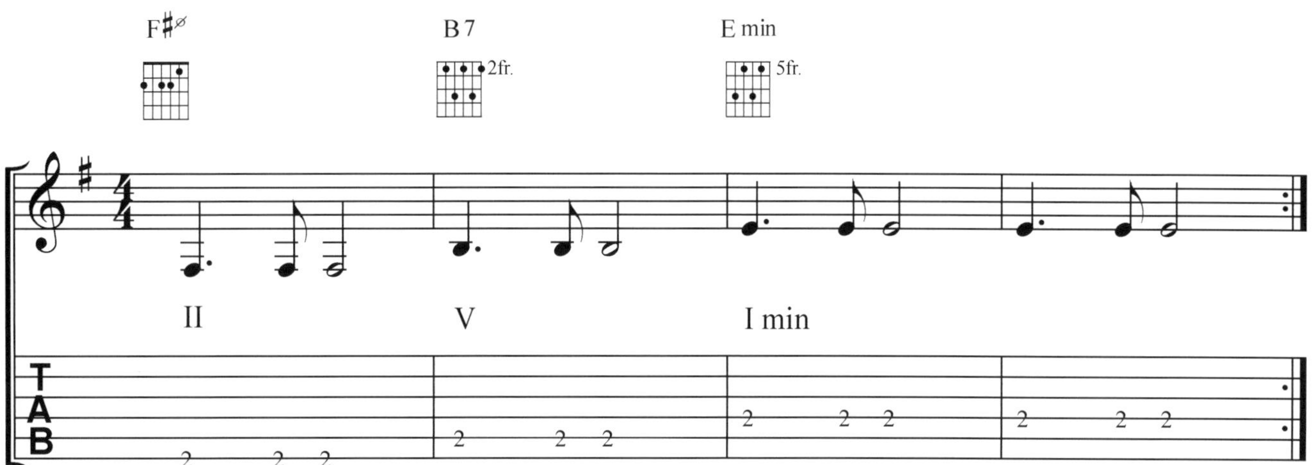

Use Emin diatonic for lead.

Diatonic Studies

G=Emin

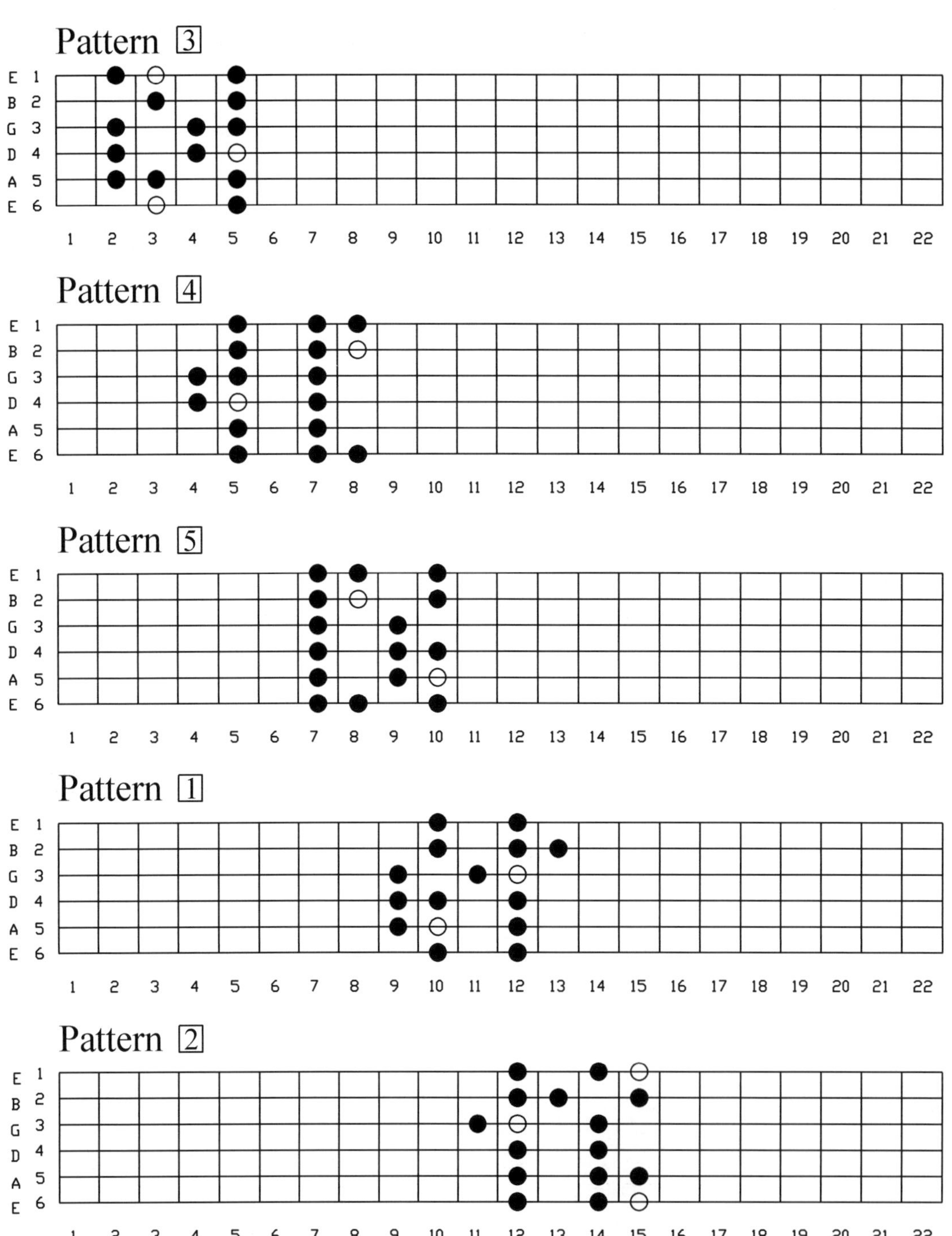

○ ROOT NOTE OF SCALE

Cycle of 5ths Progression

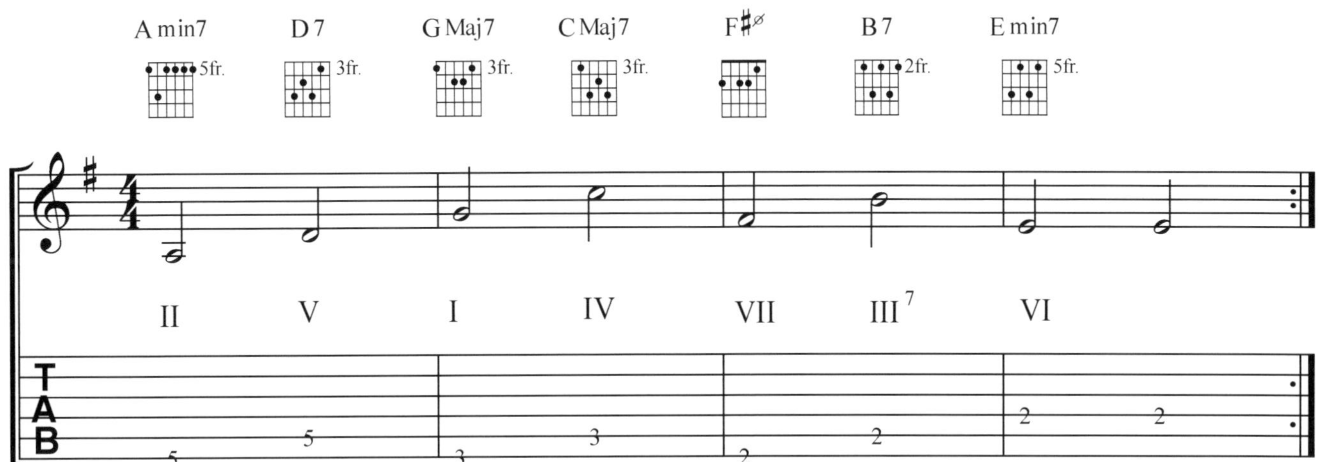

Use GMaj (Emin) diatonic scale for lead.

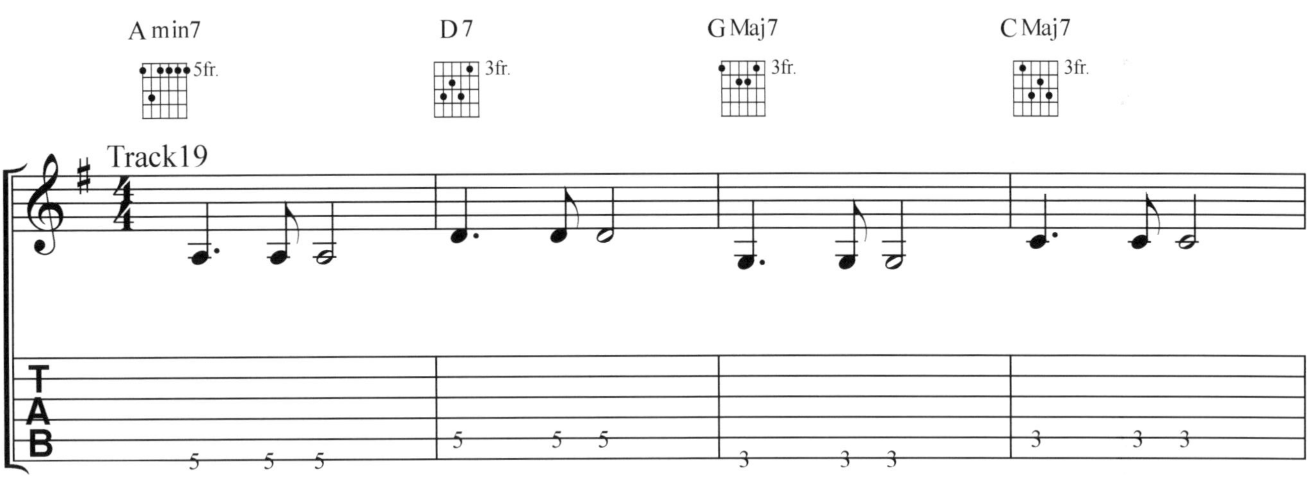

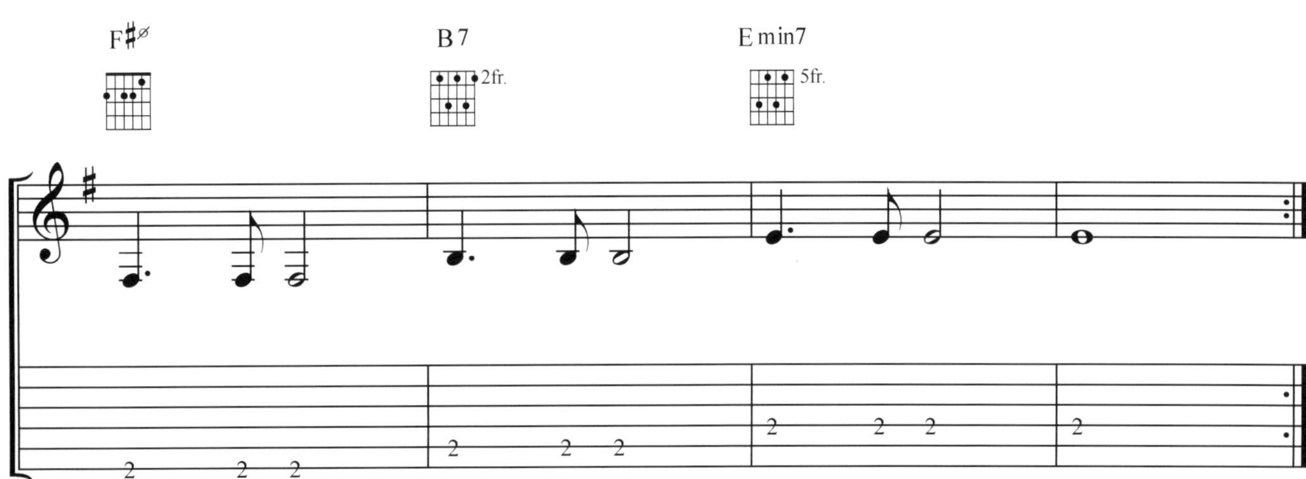

The Pentatonic Scale
Key of Dmin

Common Progressions

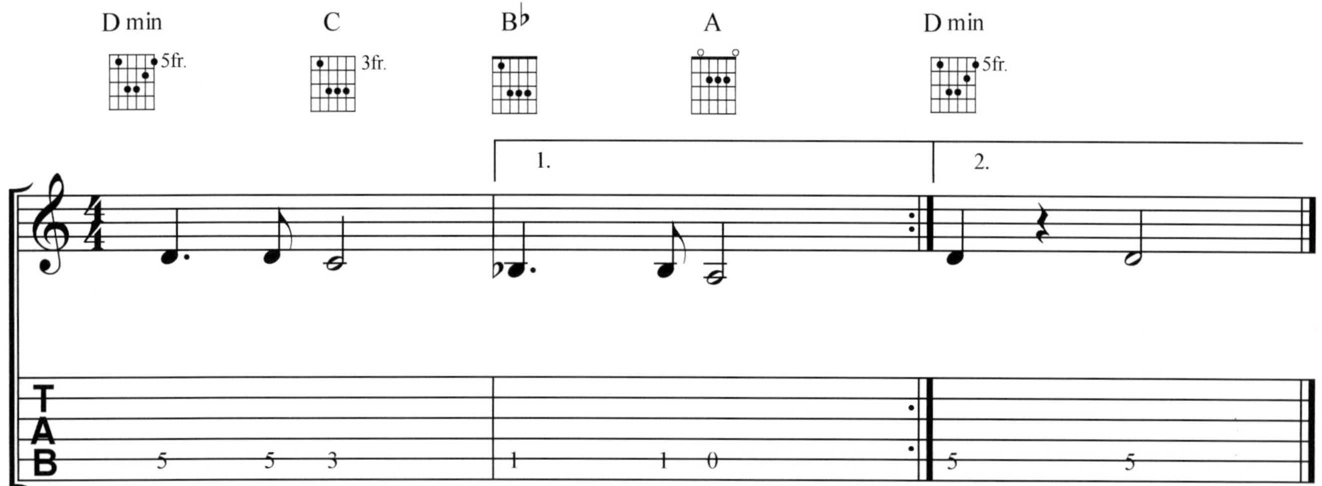

Latin Rock

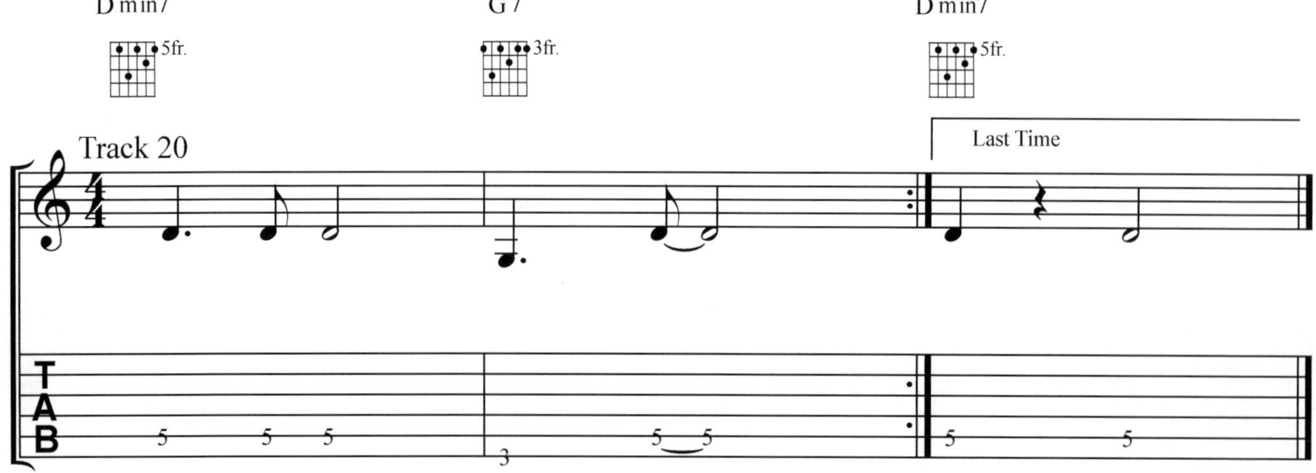

12 Bar Blues

D7
3fr.
Track 21
G7
3fr.
D7
3fr.
A7
5fr.
G7
3fr.
D7
3fr.
A7
5fr.
D7
3fr.
1.
2.

Scale Studies
Dmin Pentatonic

These are 5 different patterens at 5 positions on the fingerboard. Memorize them all and learn to shift from one to another.

D min7
10fr.
Pattern 2
T
A
B
13 10
13 10
12 10
12 10
12 10
13 10
10
10
10
10
12
10

D min7
12fr.
Pattern 3
T
A
B
13 15
12 15
12 15
12 14
13 15
13 15
13
13
14
12

Dmin

Pentatonic Studies

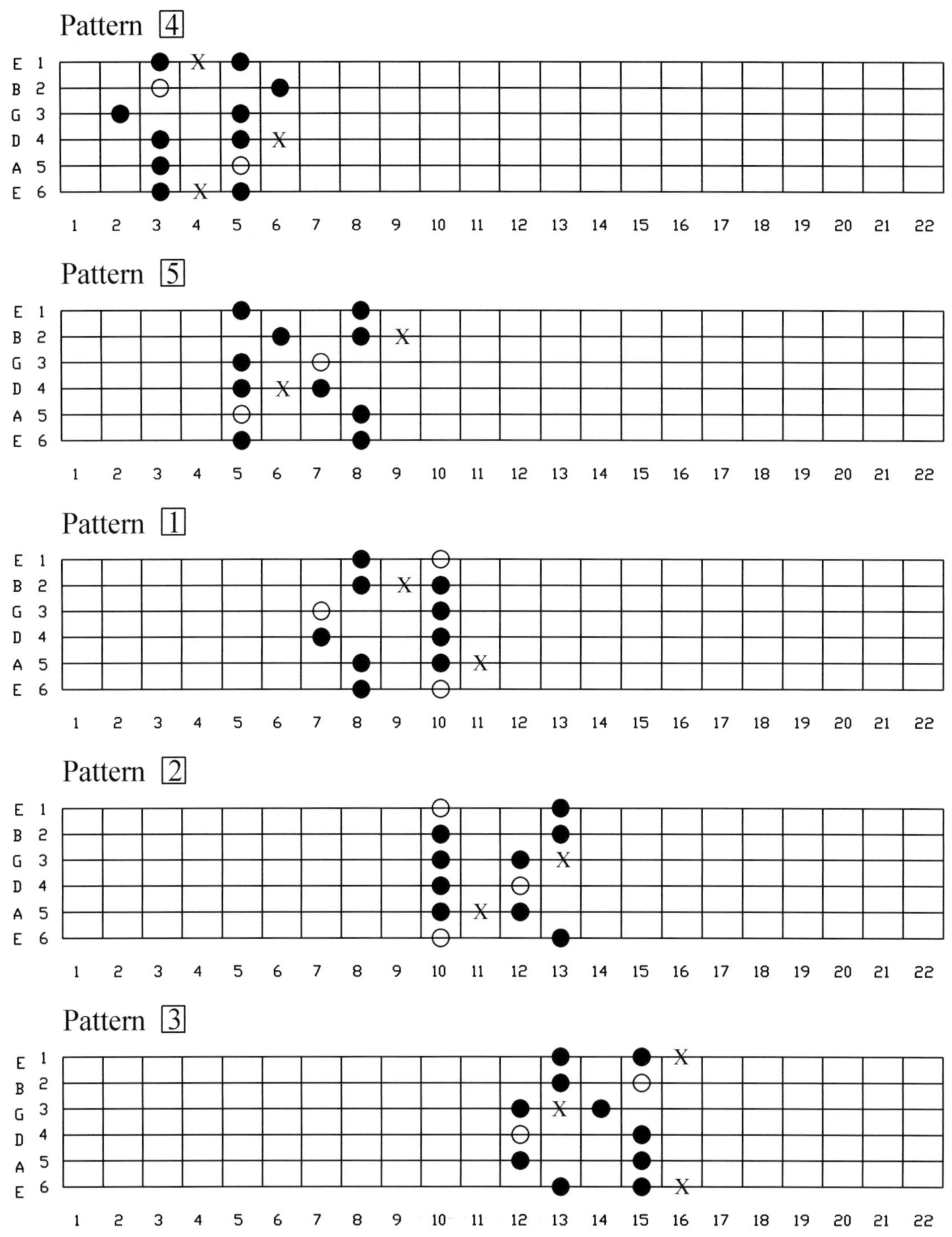

○ ROOT NOTE OF SCALE

X ADDS A FLATTED 5TH TO THE PENTATONIC SCALE TO CREATE THE BLUES SCALE

Chords

Key Center of F

The FMaj pentatonic scale is equal to the Dmin pentatonic scale. They share the same notes and are said to be enharmonic equivalents. So, use all 5 Dmin pentatonic patterns to play over this FMaj progression.

Scale Studies
F = Dmin Diatonic

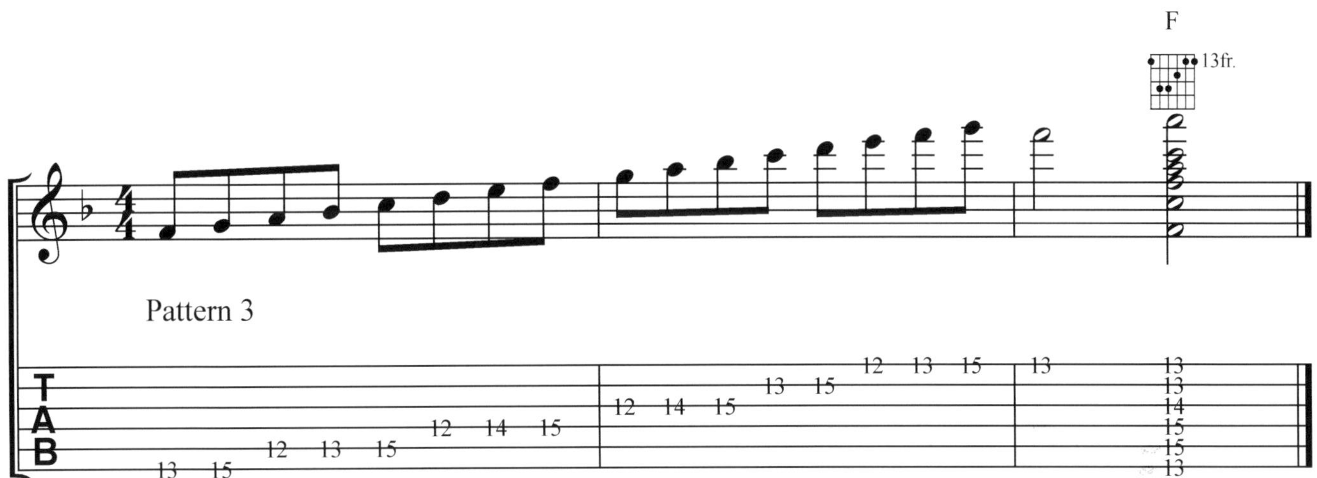

Common Progression

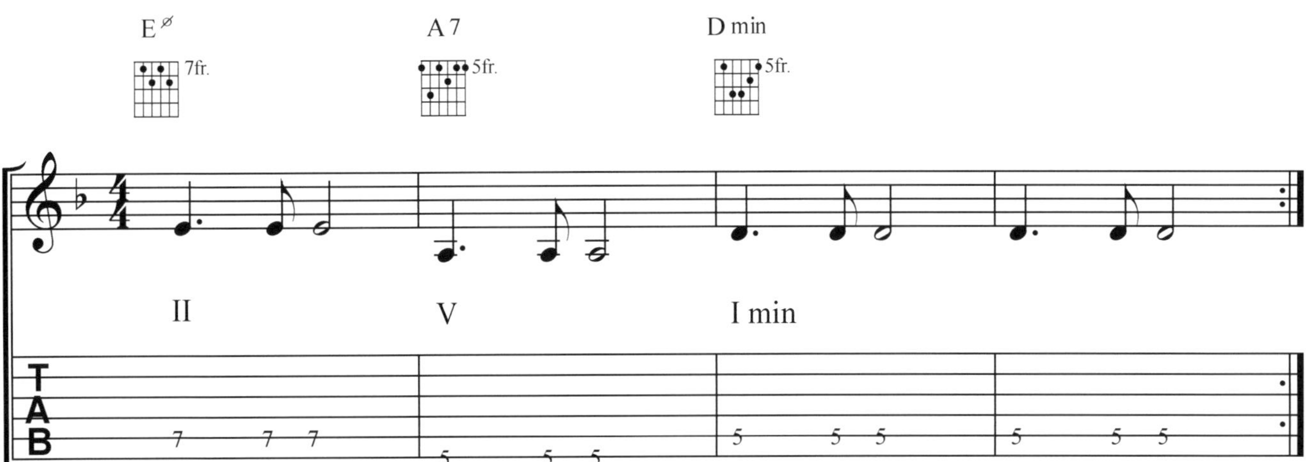

Use Dmin diatonic for lead.

Diatonic Studies

F=Dmin

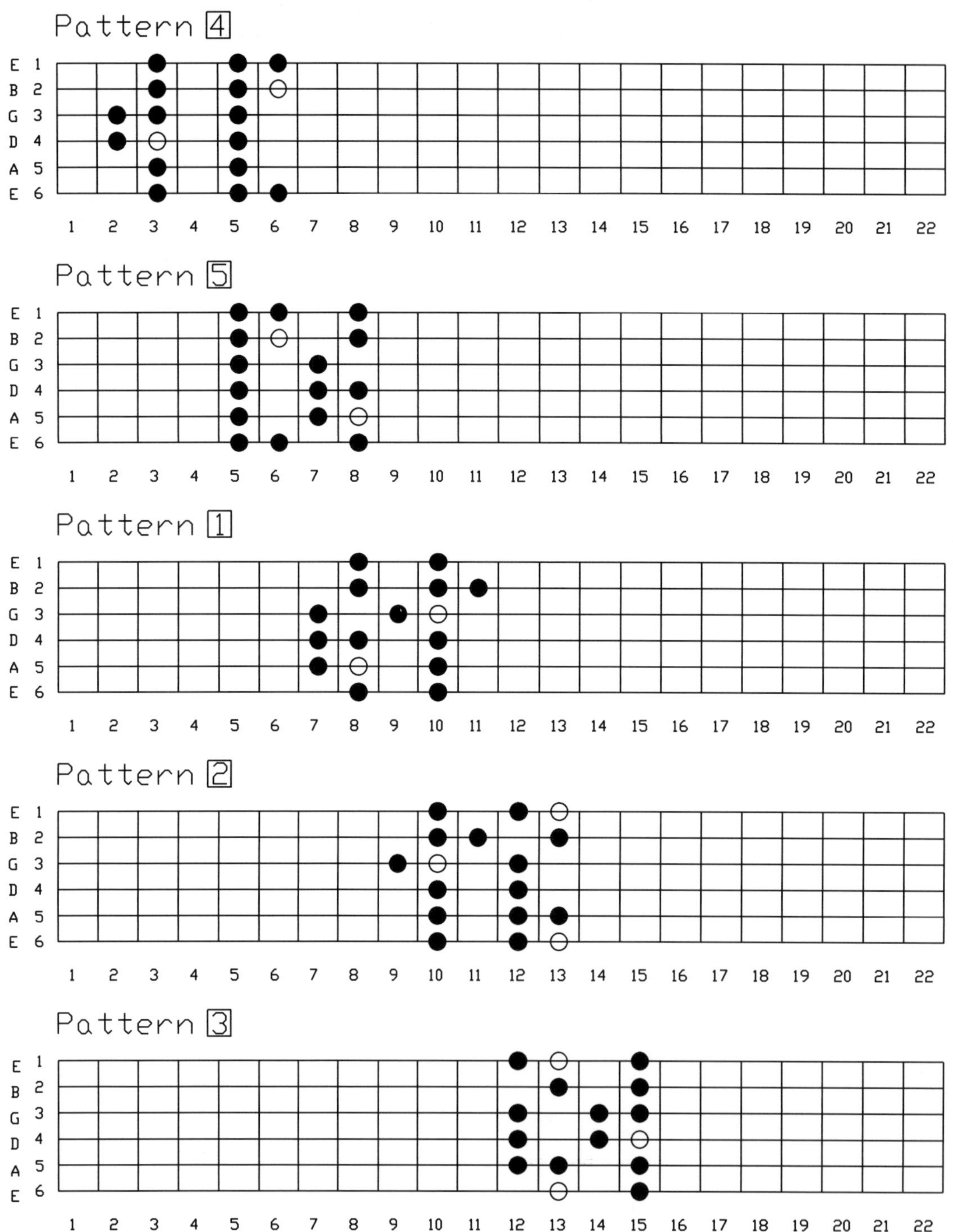

○ ROOT NOTE OF SCALE

Cycle of 5ths Progression

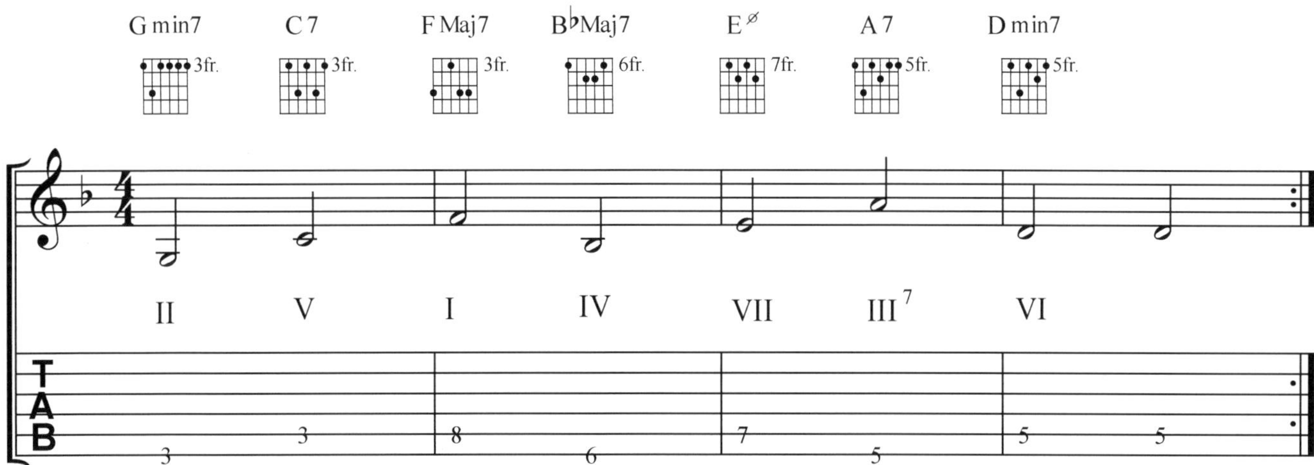

Use FMaj (Dmin) diatonic scale for lead.

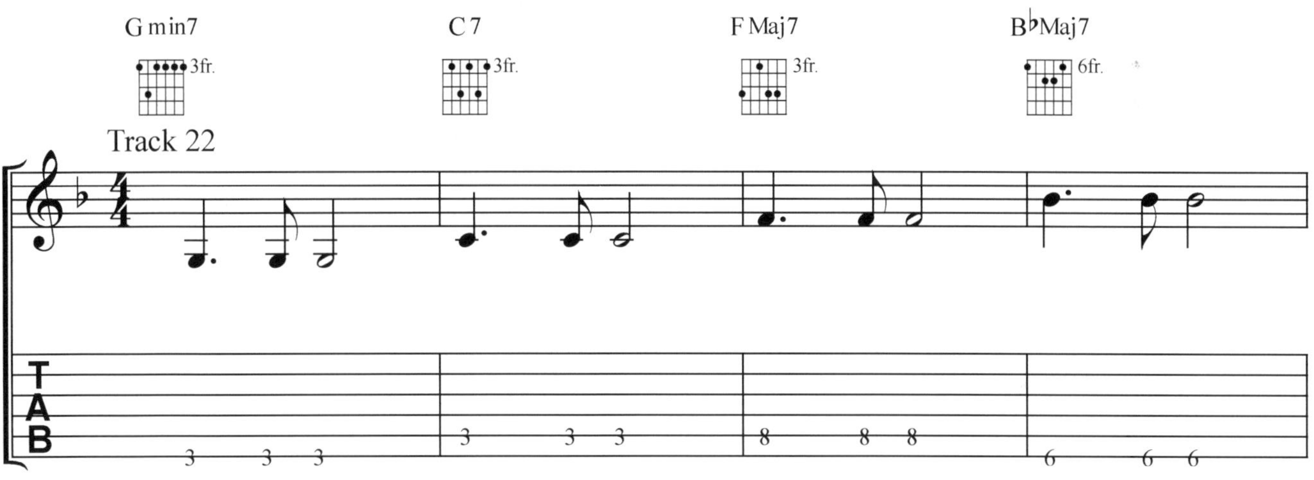

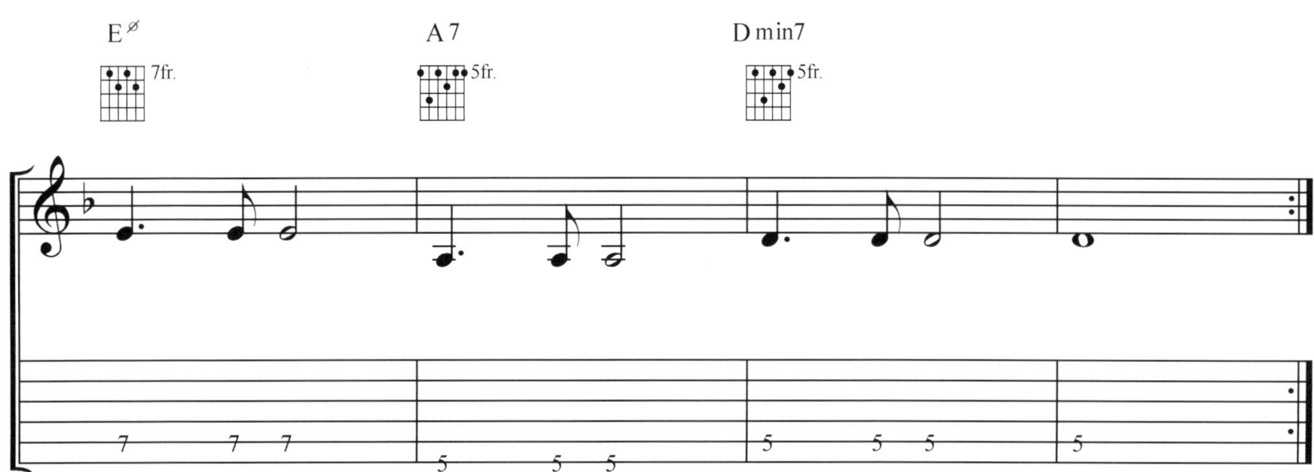

The Pentatonic Scale
Key of Fmin

Common Progressions

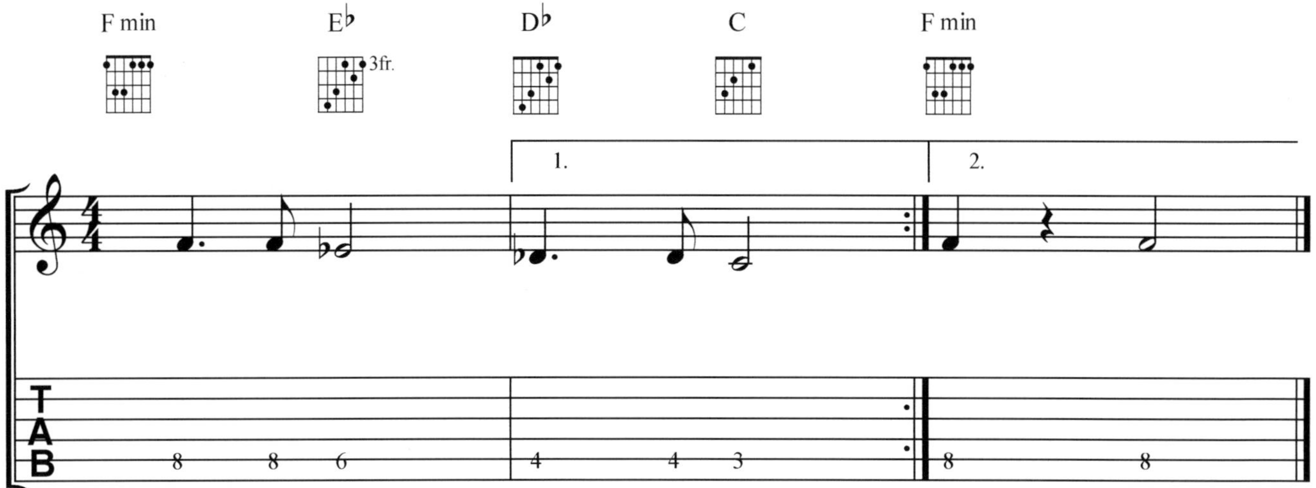

Latin Rock

12 Bar Blues

F7
6fr.
Track 24
Bb7
6fr.
F7
6fr.
C7
8fr.
Bb7
6fr.
F7
6fr.
C7
8fr.
F7
6fr.
1.
2.

Scale Studies
Fmin Pentatonic

These are 5 different patterns at 5 positions on the fingerboard. Memorize them all and learn to shift from one to another.

F min7
13fr.
Pattern 1
13 11 13 11 13 10 13 10
13 11 13 11
13 13 13 13

F min7
13fr.
Pattern 2
13 16 13 15 13 15 13 15
13 16 13 16
13 13 13 13 15 13

Fmin
Pentatonic Studies

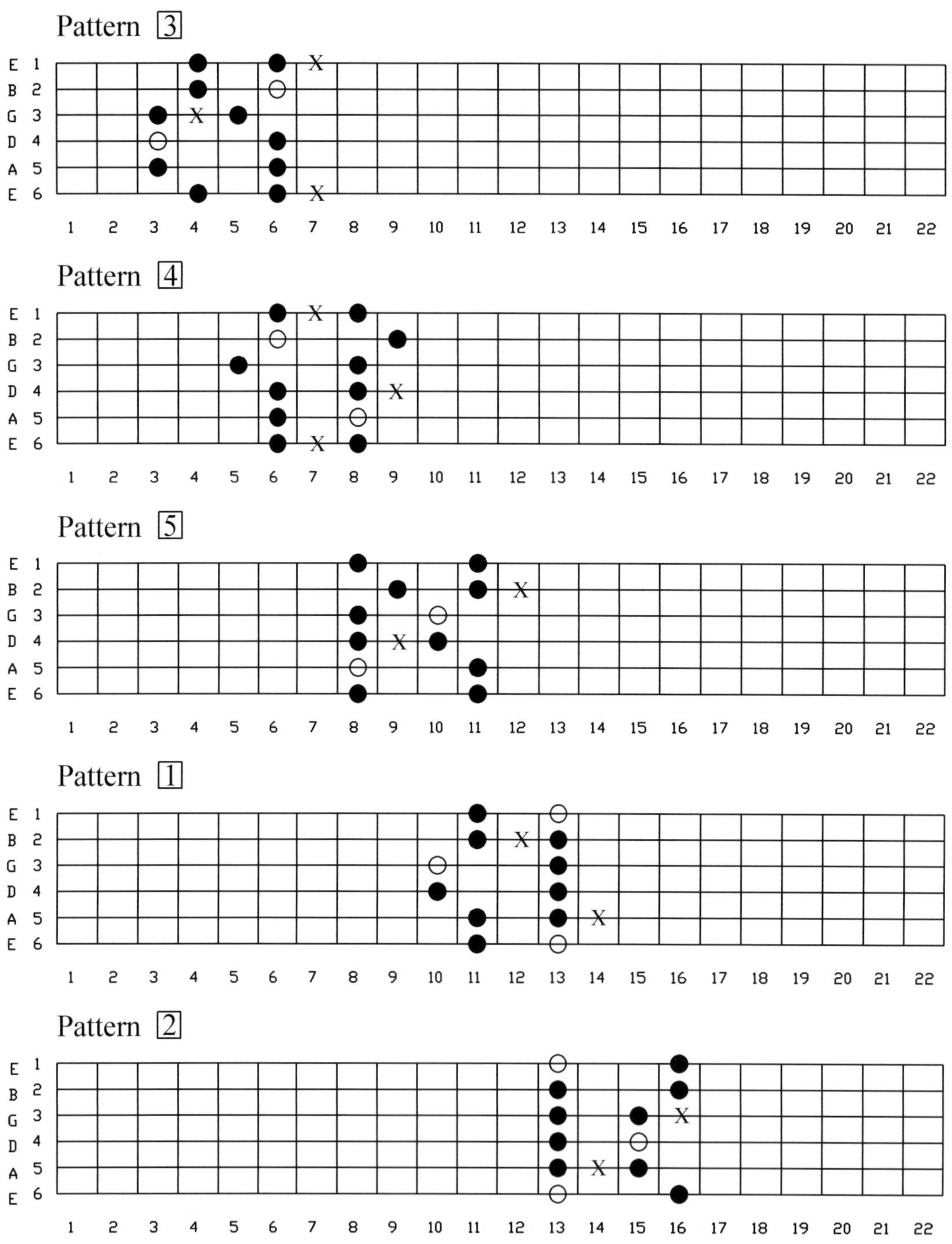

○ ROOT NOTE OF SCALE

X ADDS A FLATTED 5TH TO THE PENTATONIC SCALE TO CREATE THE BLUES SCALE

Chords

Key Center of Ab

The AbMaj pentatonic scale is equal to the Fmin pentatonic scale. They share the same notes and are said to be enharmonic equivalents. So, use all 5 Fmin pentatonic patterns to play over this AbMaj progression.

Scale Studies
Ab = Fmin Diatonic

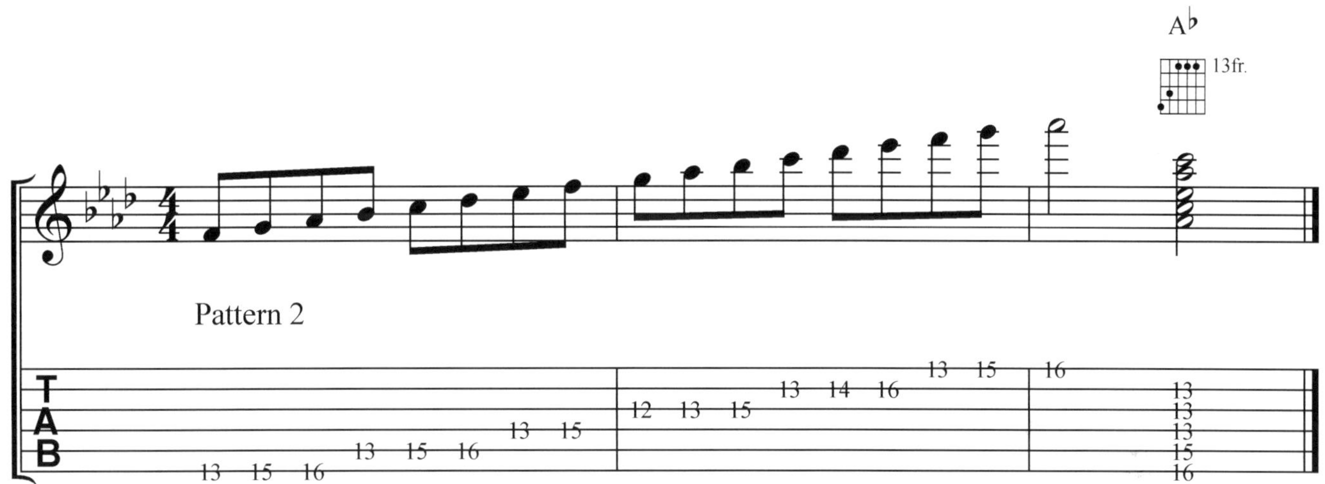

Common Progression

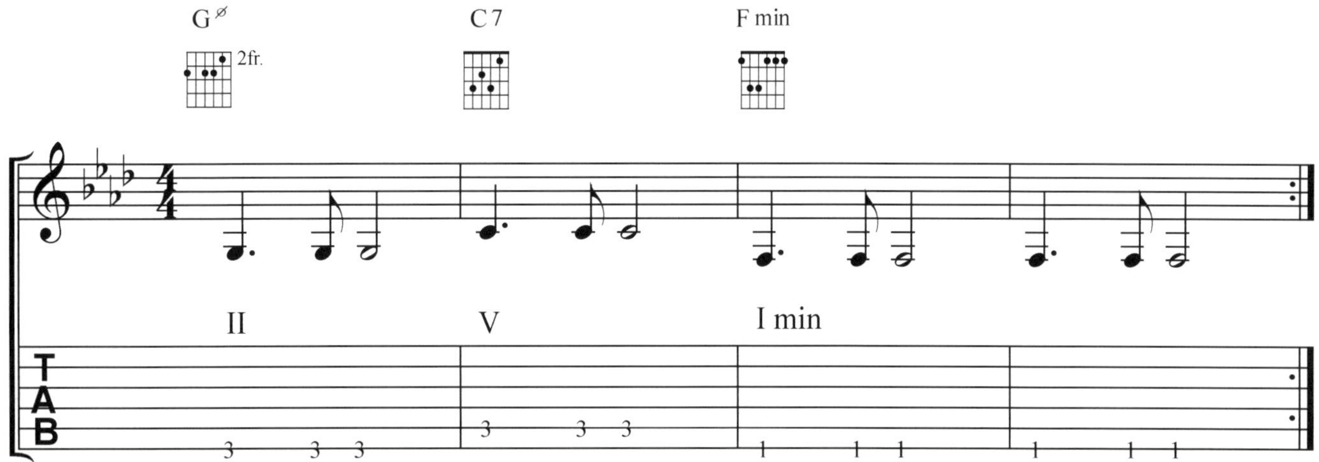

Use Fmin diatonic for lead.

Diatonic Studies

Ab=Fmin

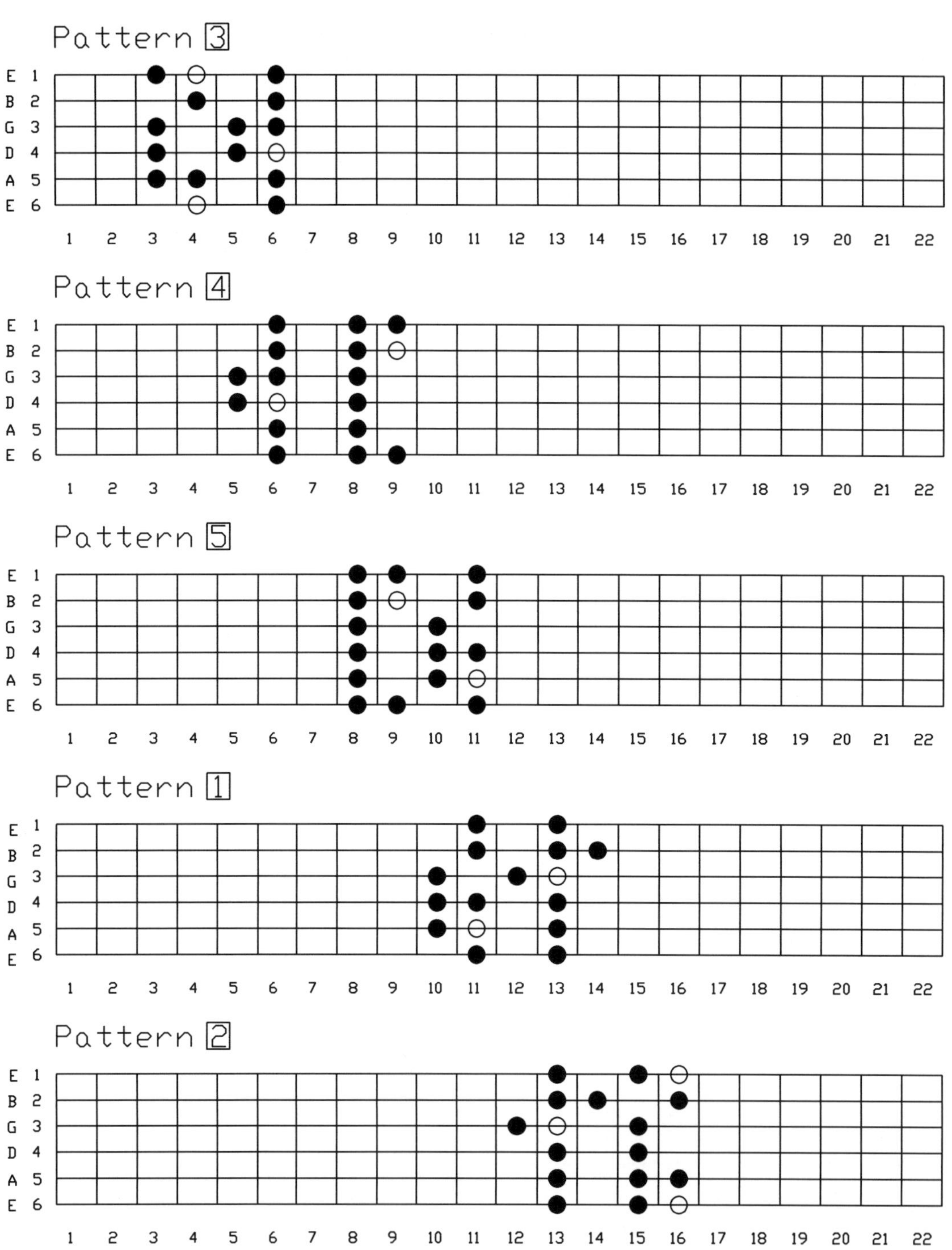

○ ROOT NOTE OF SCALE

Cycle of 5ths Progression

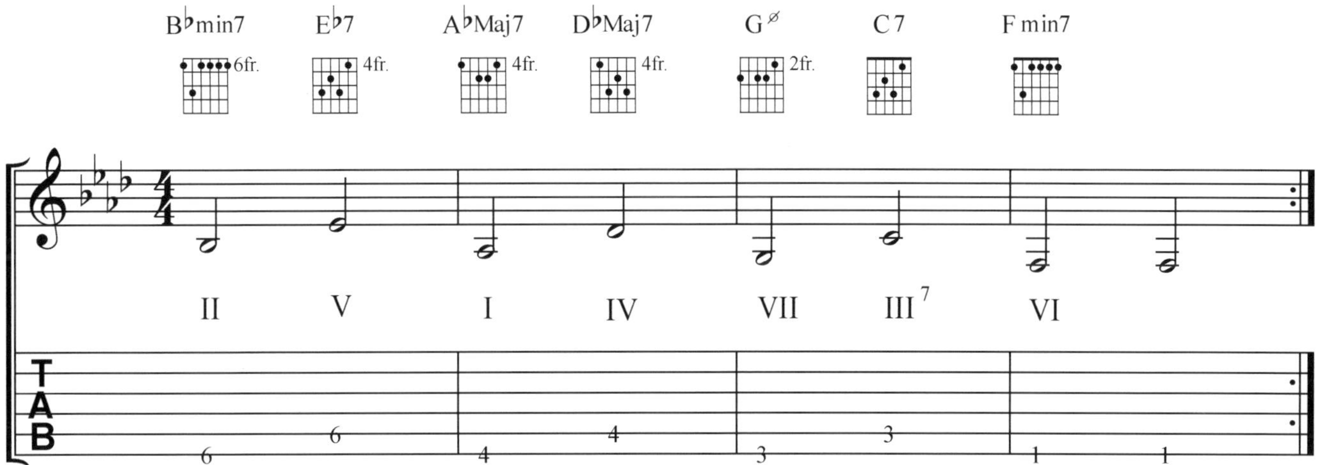

Use AbMaj (Fmin) diatonic scale for lead.

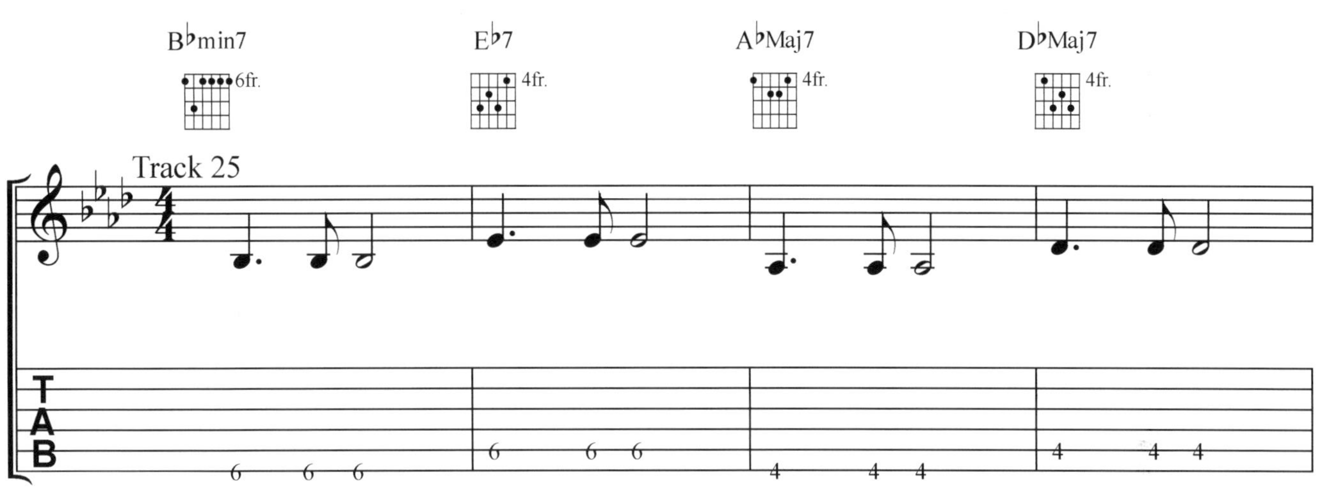

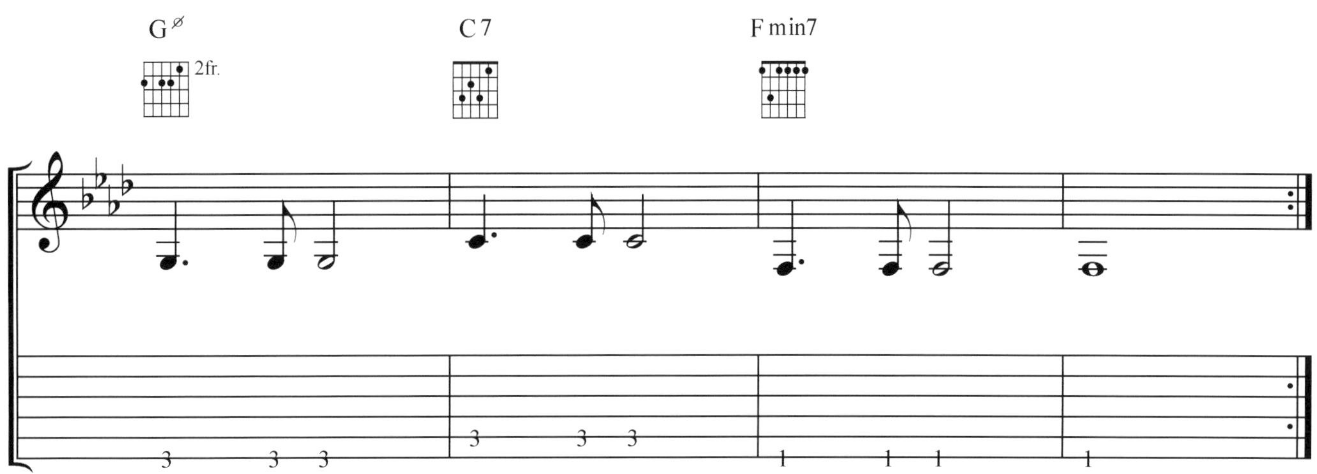

Finding Key Center
Arpeggio Study

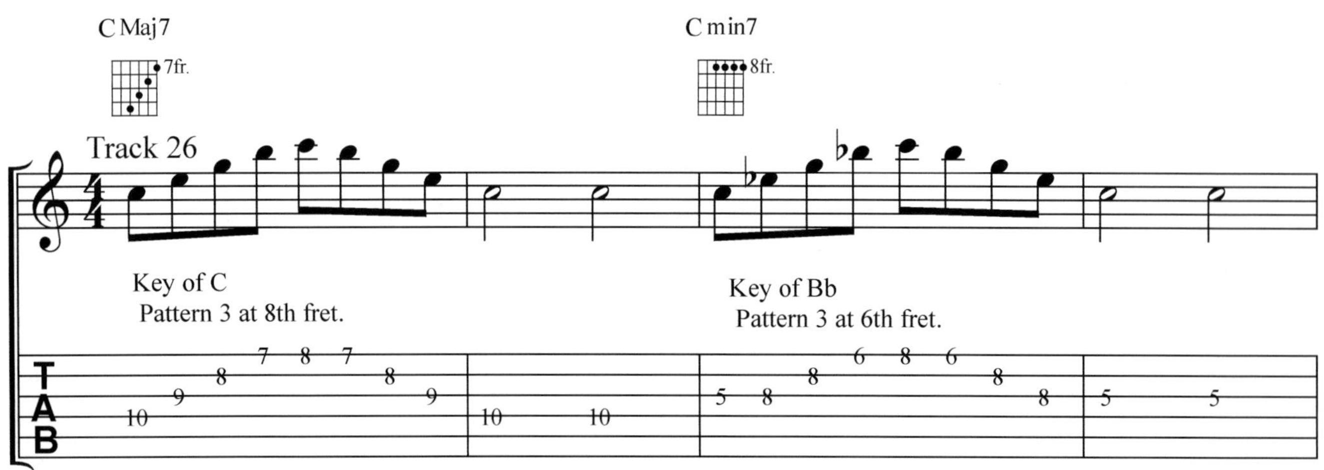

An arpeggio is the notes of a chord played one at a time.

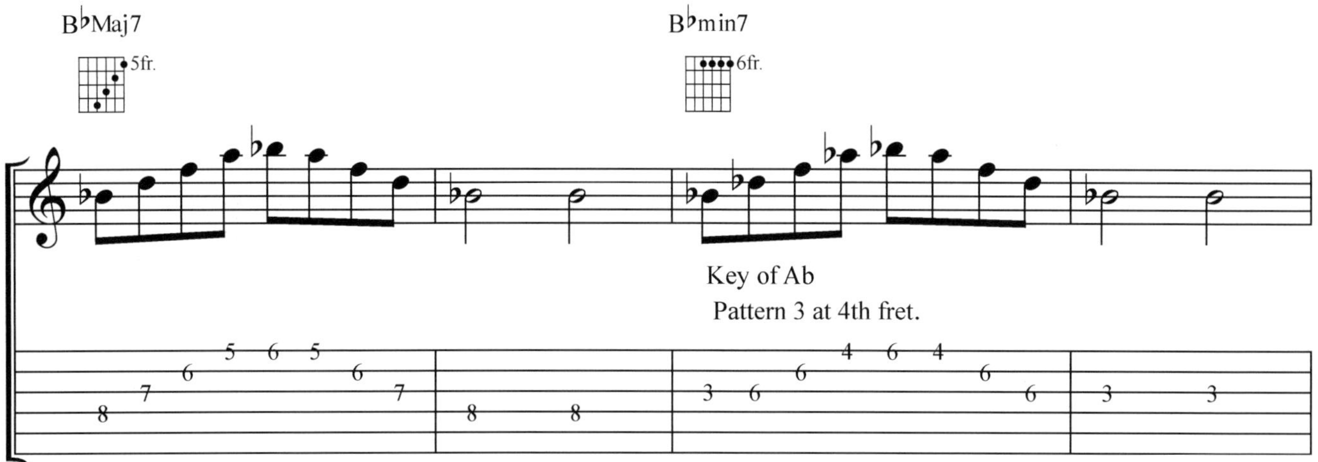

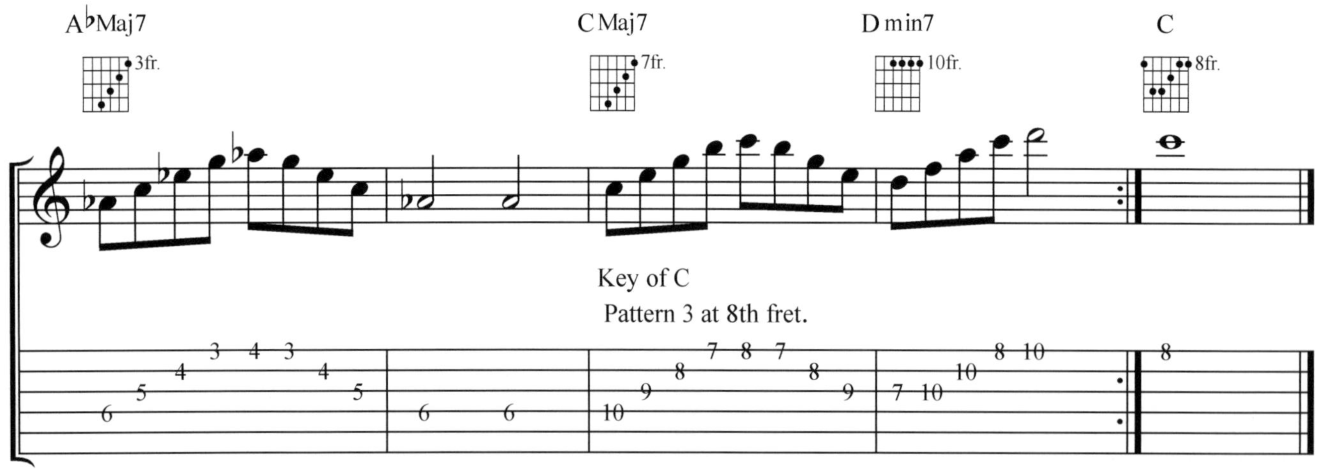

This common progression is written in the key of C . However, there are implied key modulations (changes), as it borrows chords from other keys, i.e. Cmin7 is the II chord of Bb.

Finding Key Center
Arpeggio to Scale

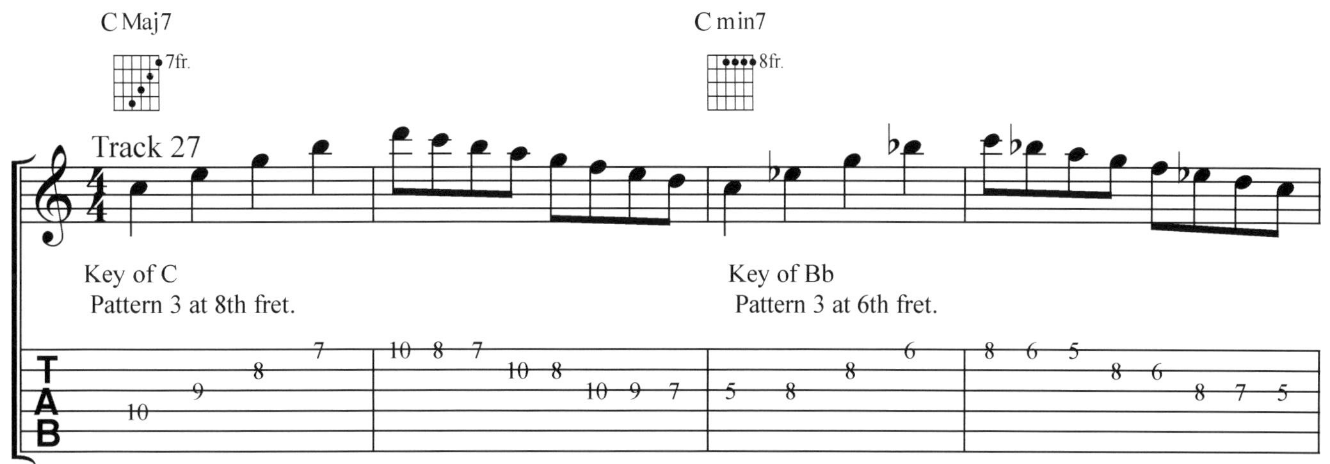

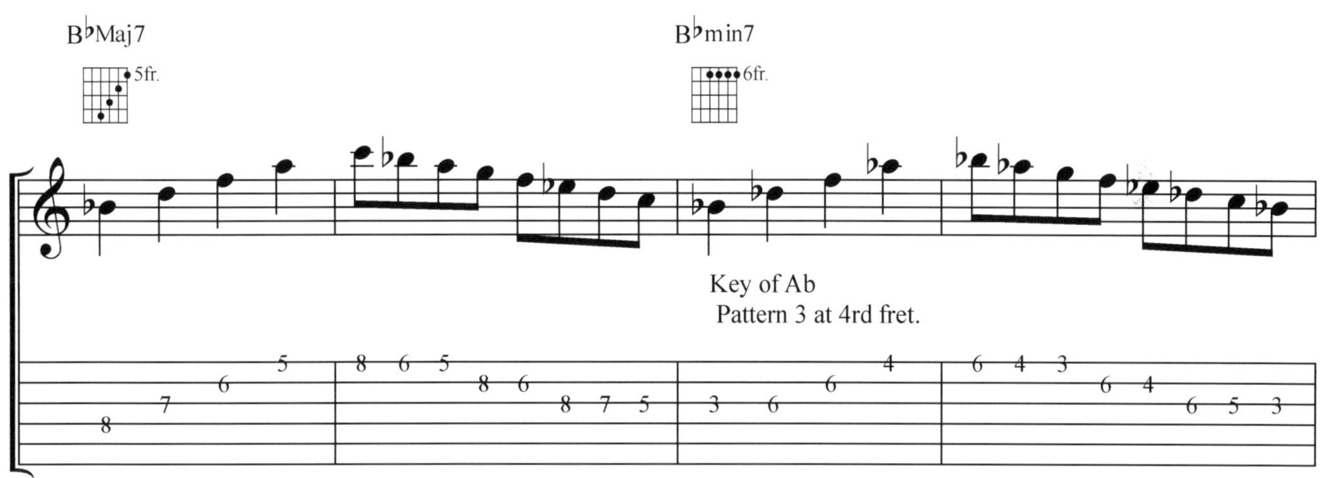

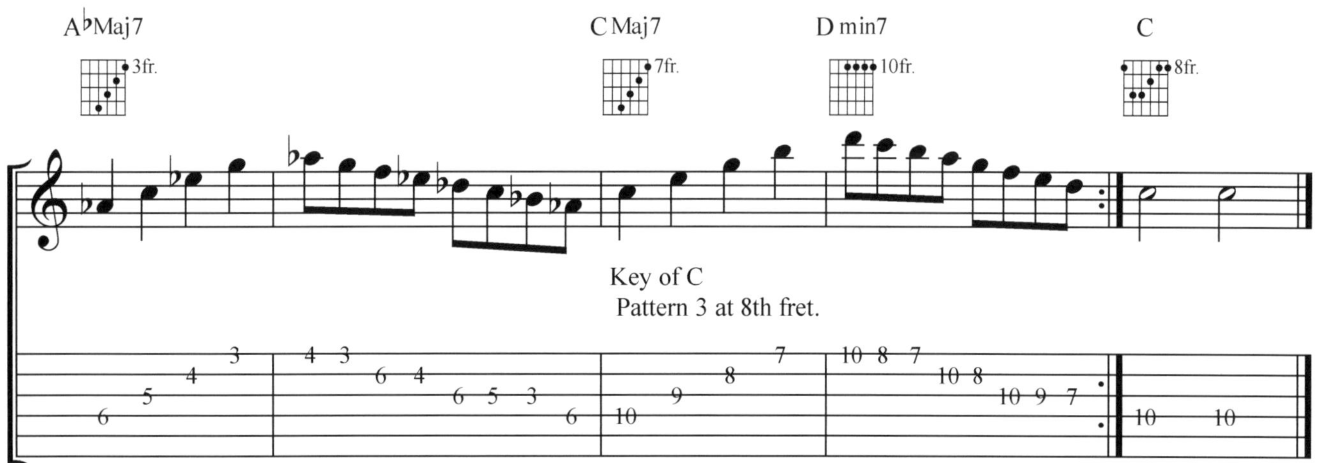

Finding Key Center
Arpeggio Study

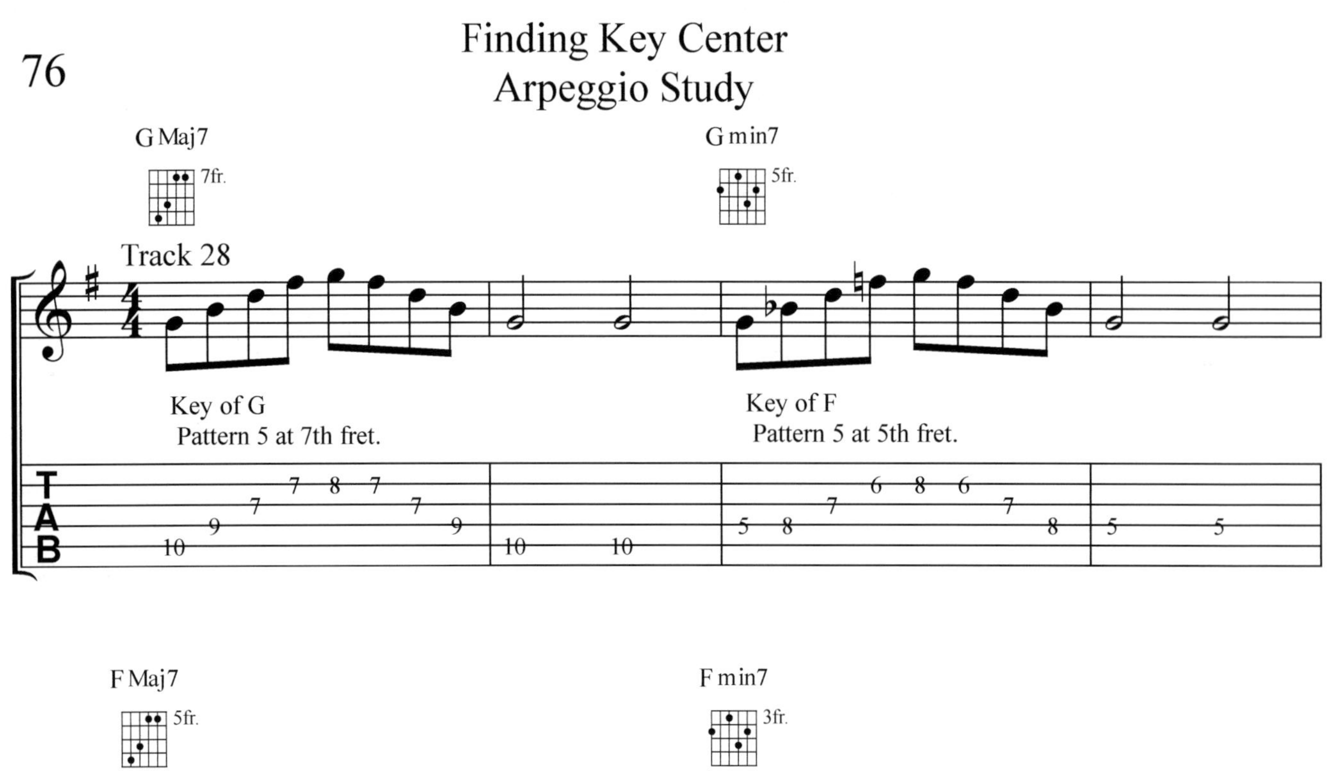

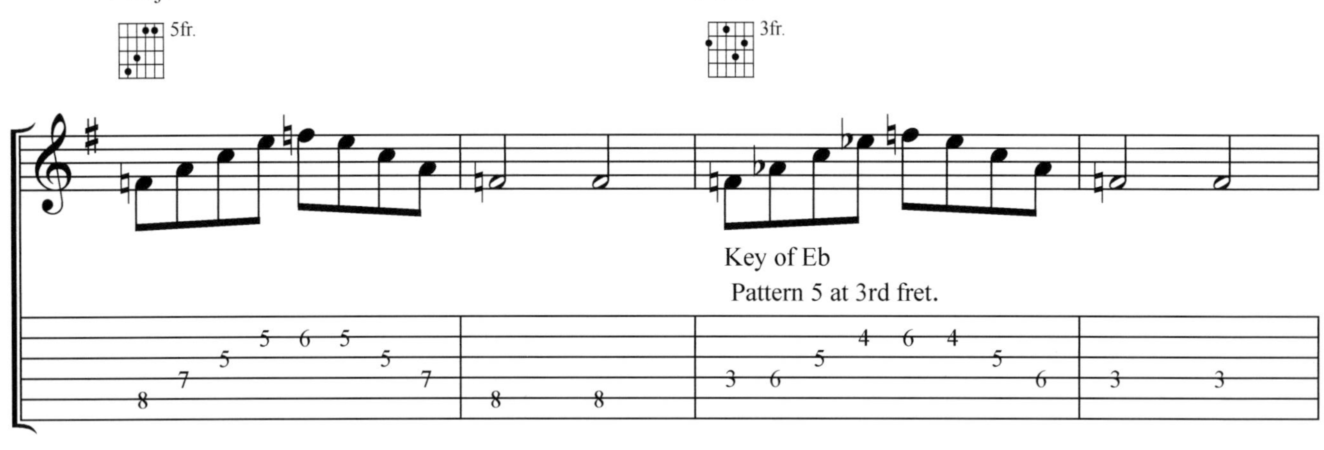

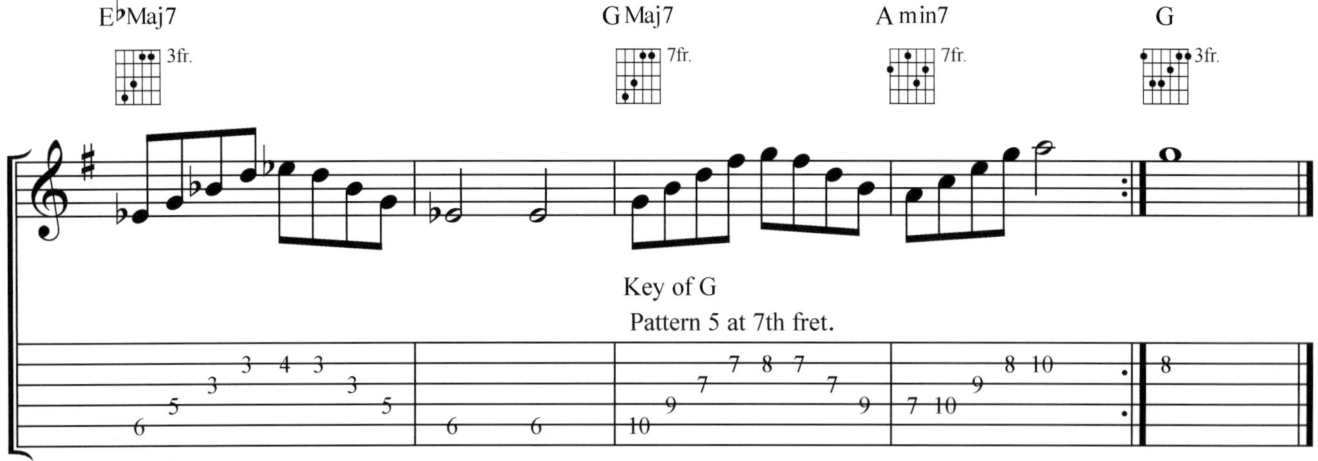

This common progression is written in the key of G (1 sharp). However, there are implied key modulations (changes), as it borrows chords from other keys, i.e. Gmin7 is the II chord of F.

Finding Key Center
Arpeggio to Scale

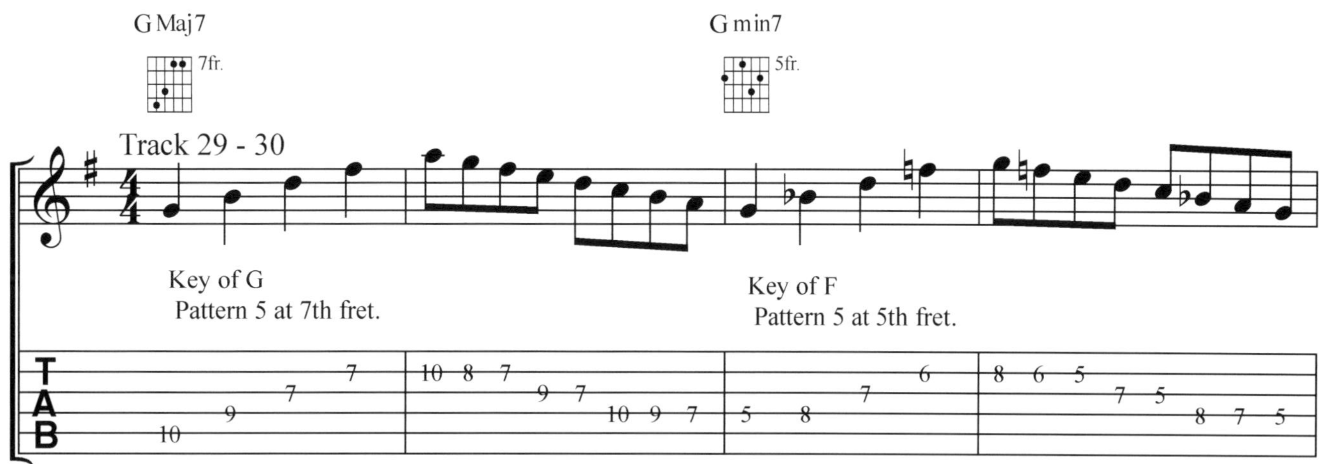

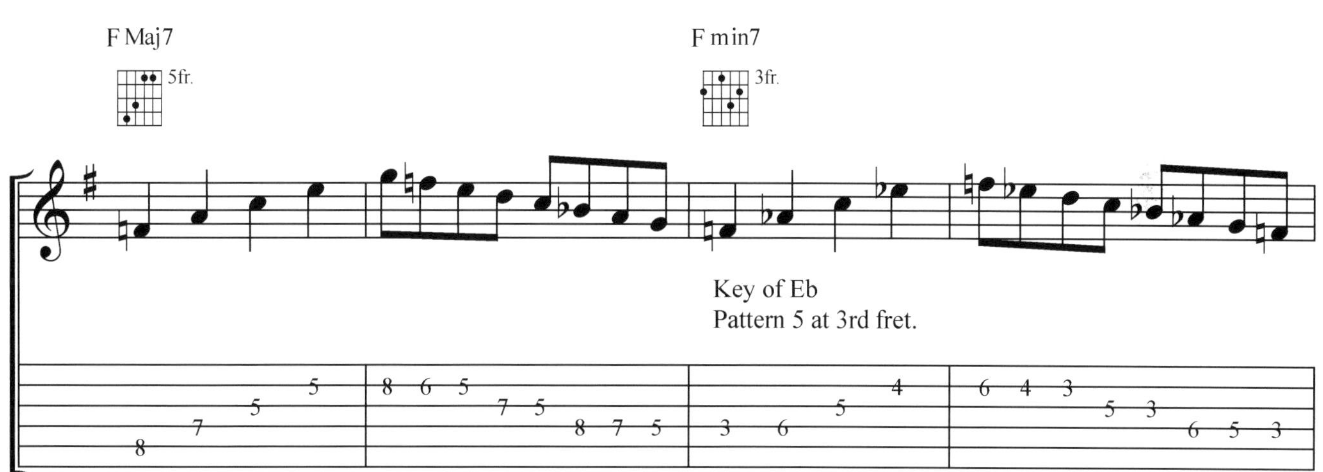

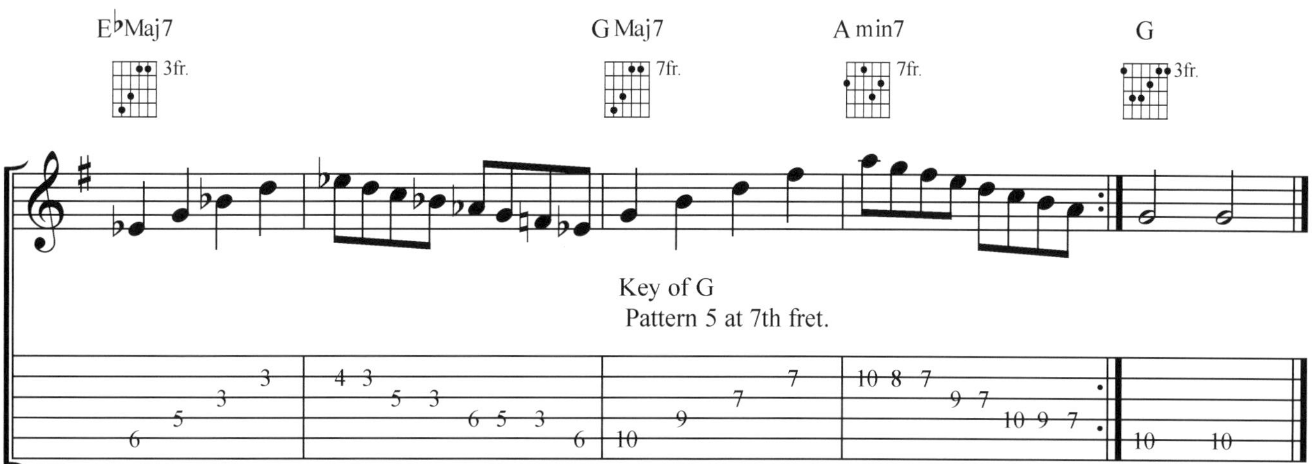

Finding Key Center
Arpeggio Study

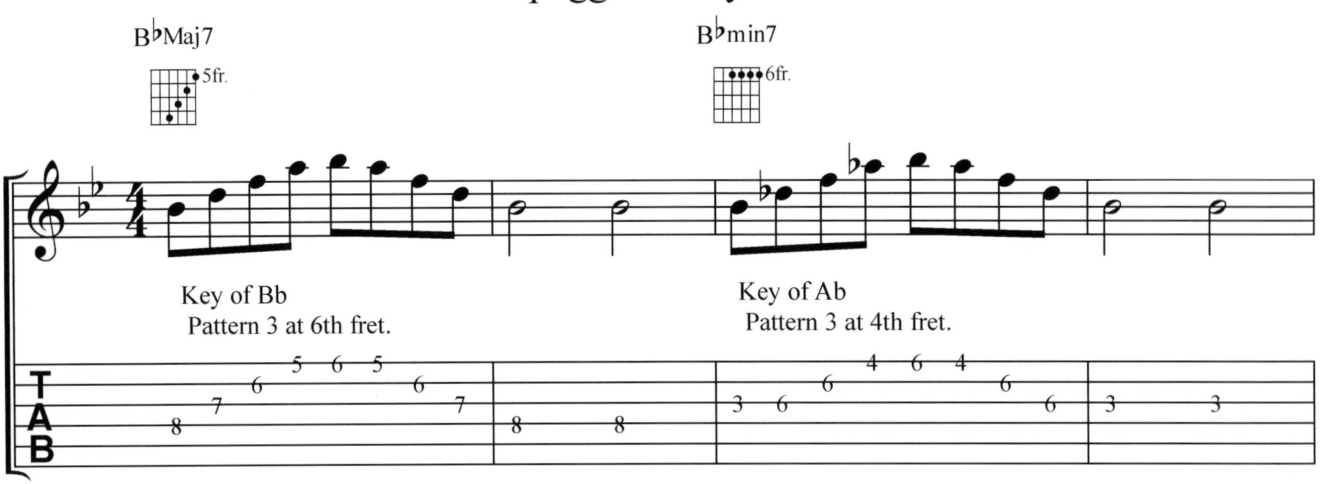

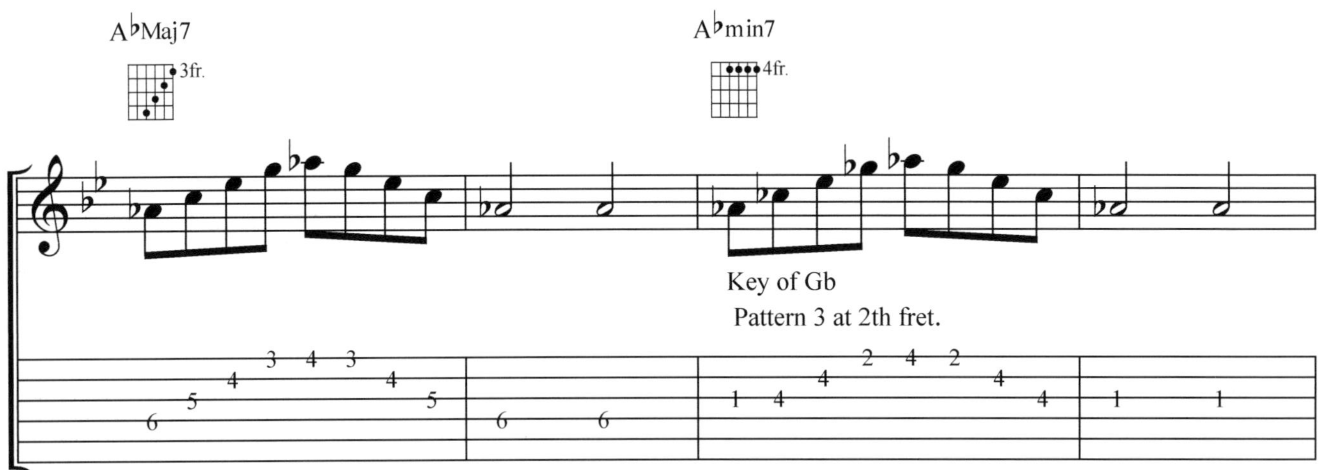

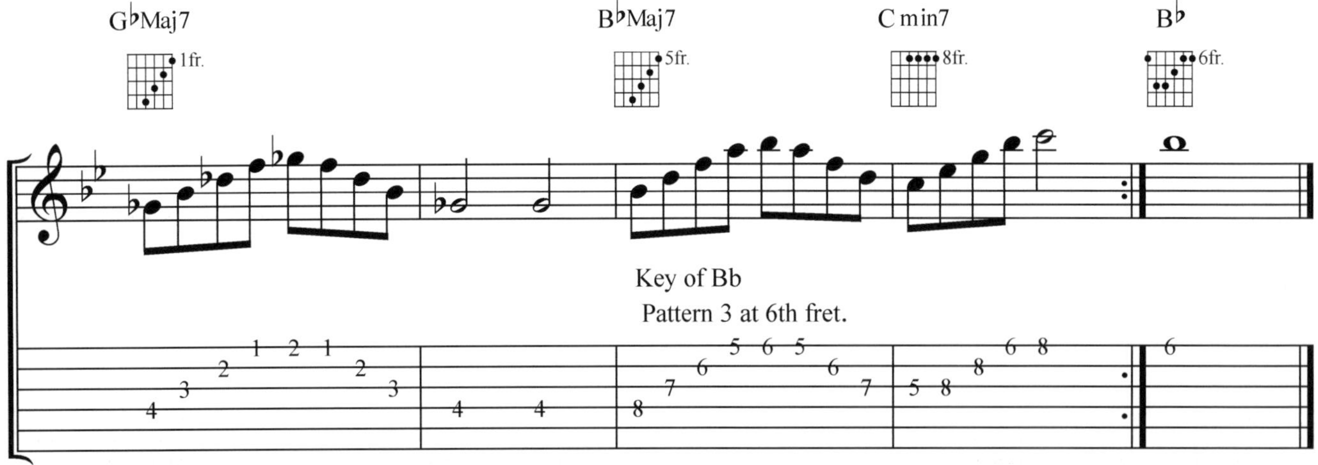

This common progression is written in the key of Bb (2 flats). However, there are implied key modulations (changes), as it borrows chords from other keys, i.e. Bbmin7 is the II chord of Ab.

Finding Key Center
Arpeggio to Scale

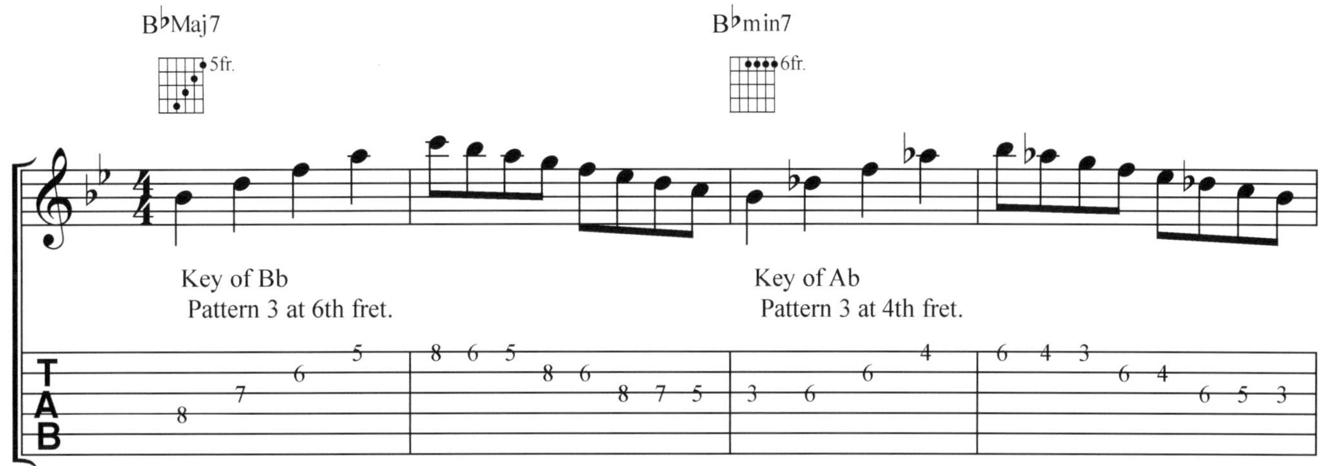

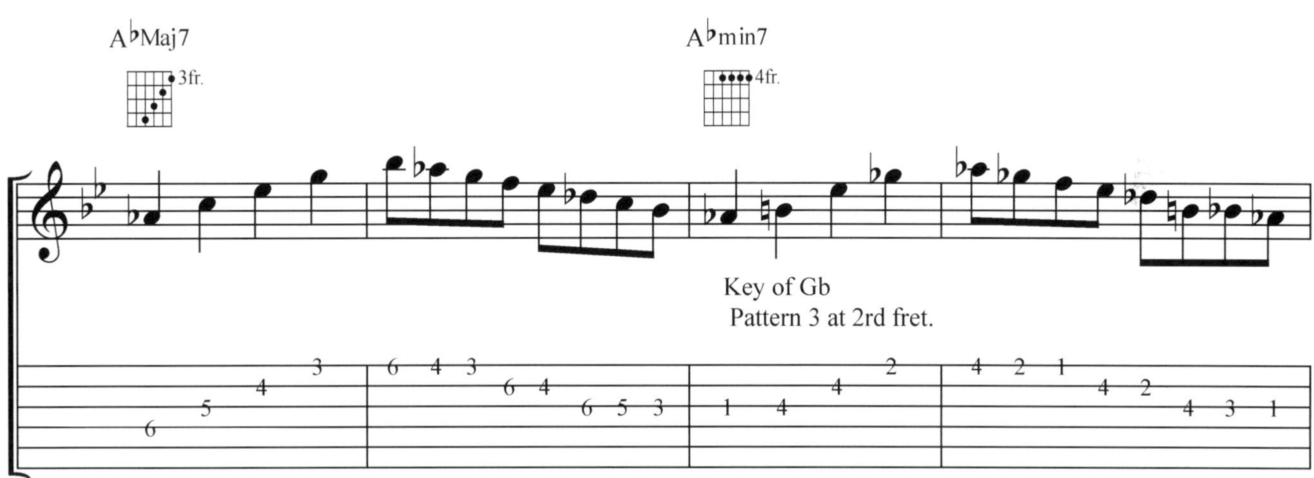

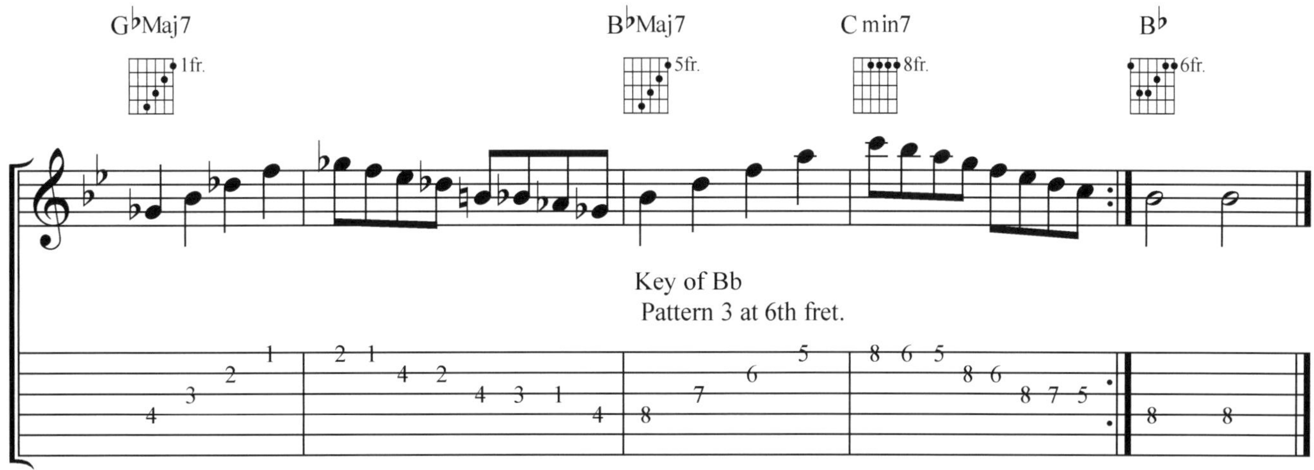

Finding Key Center
Arpeggio Study

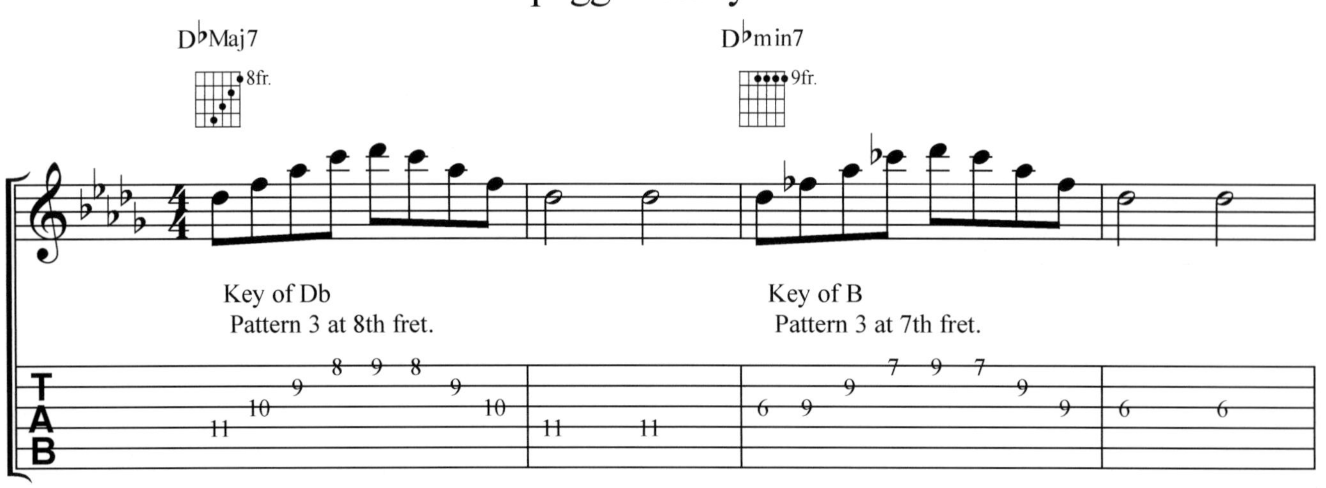

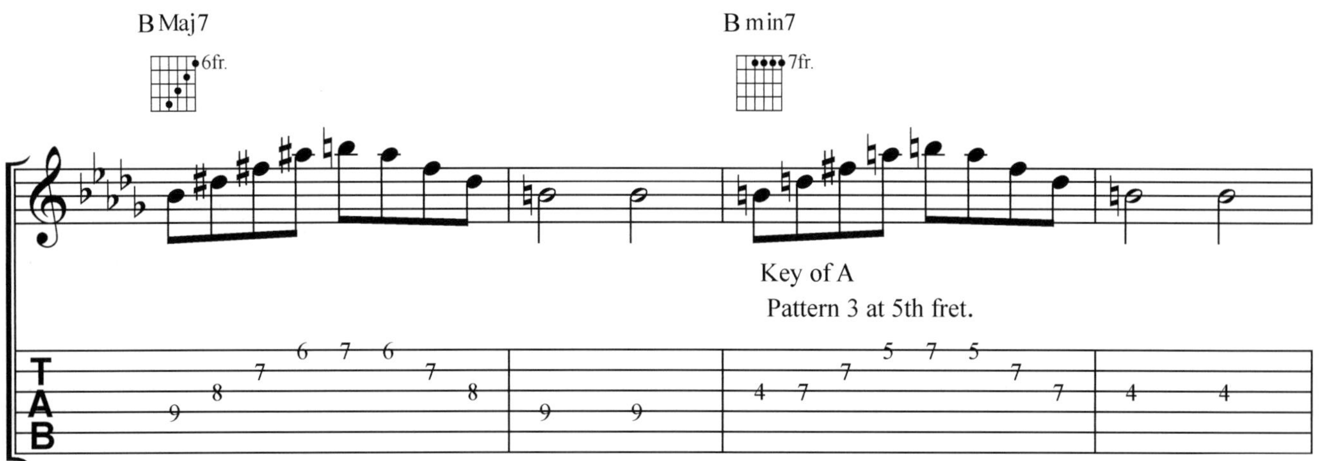

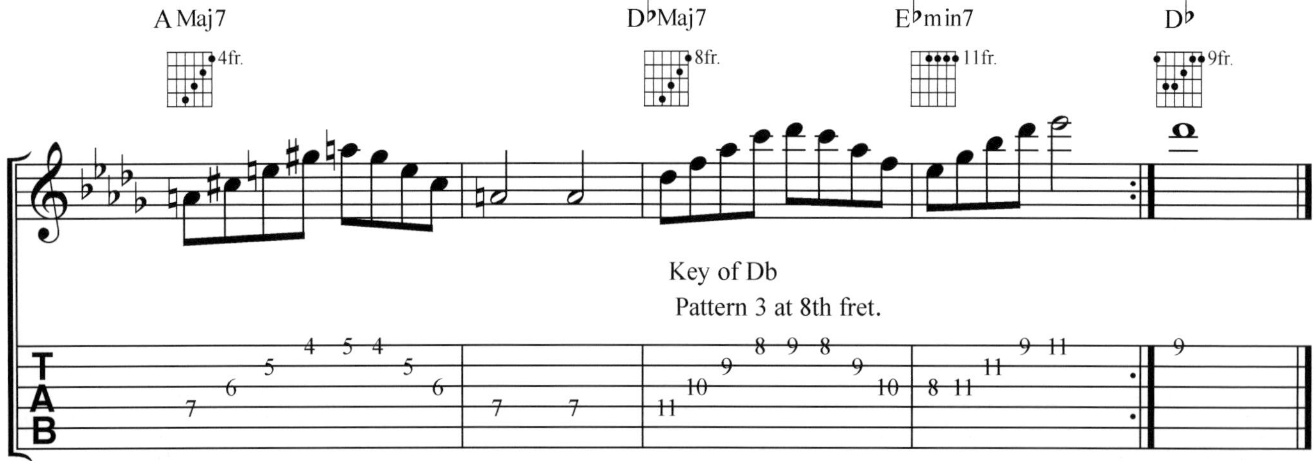

This common progression is written in the key of Db (5 flats). However, there are implied key modulations (changes), as it borrows chords from other keys, i.e. Dbmin7 which is equivalent to a C#min7, is the II chord of B.

Finding Key Center
Arpeggio to Scale

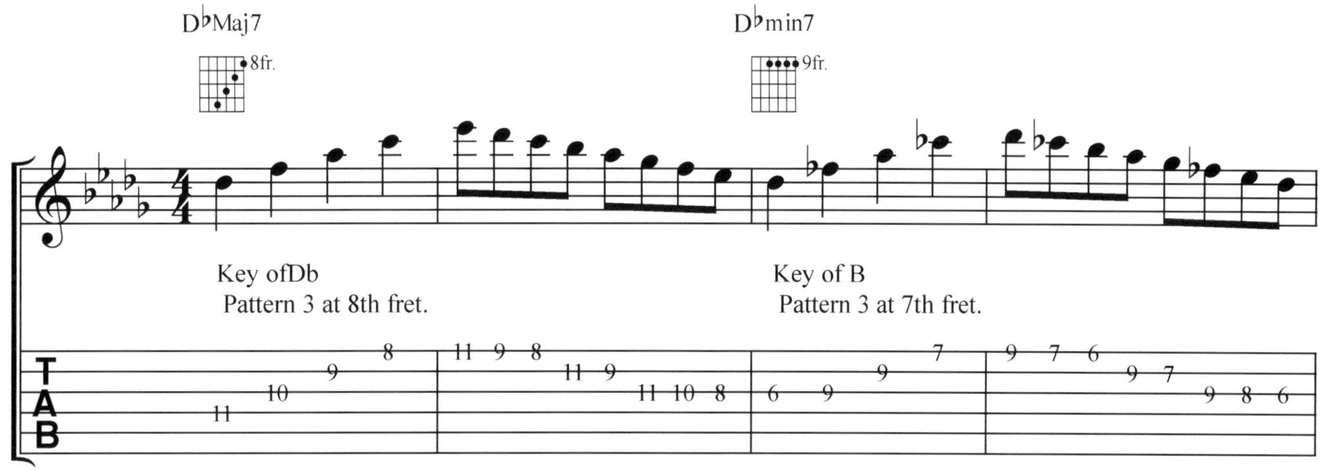

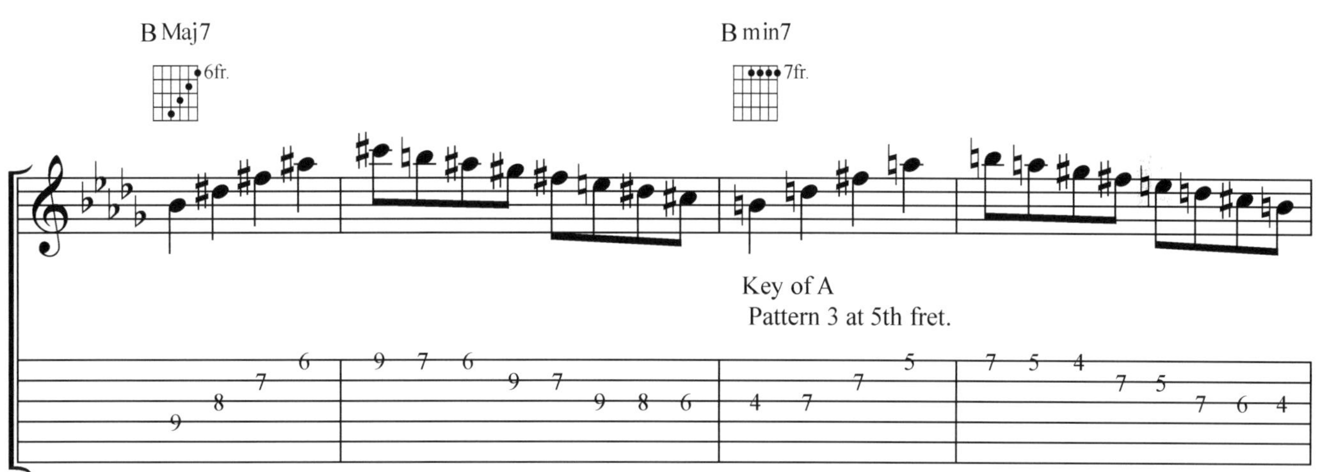

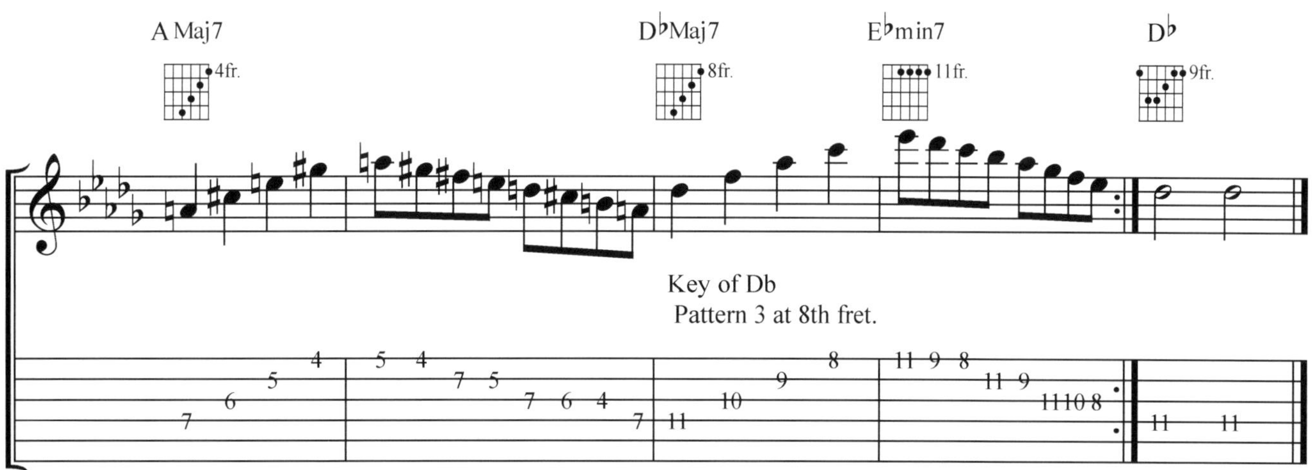

Finding Key Center
Arpeggio Study

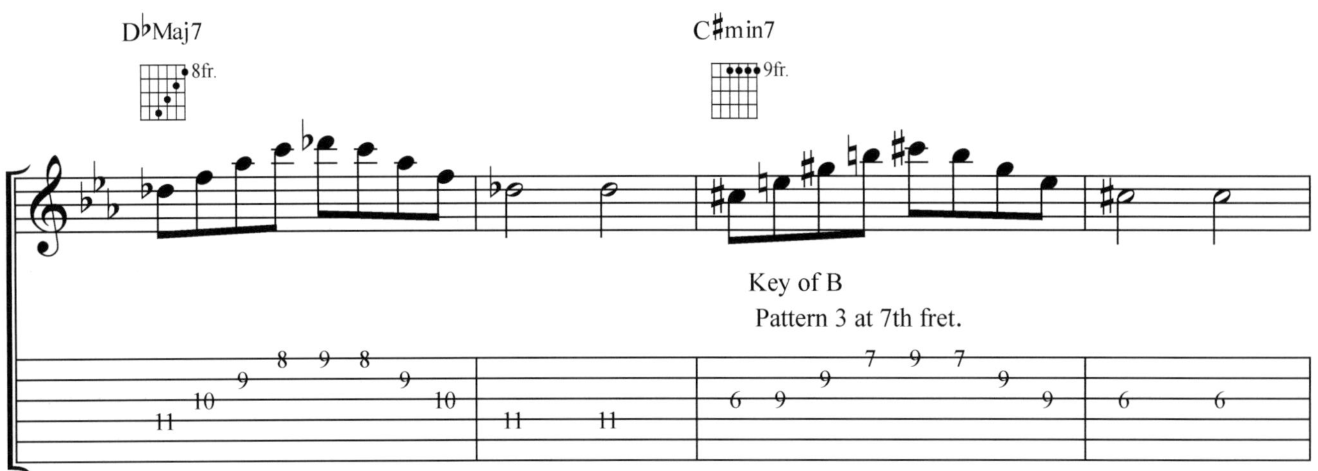

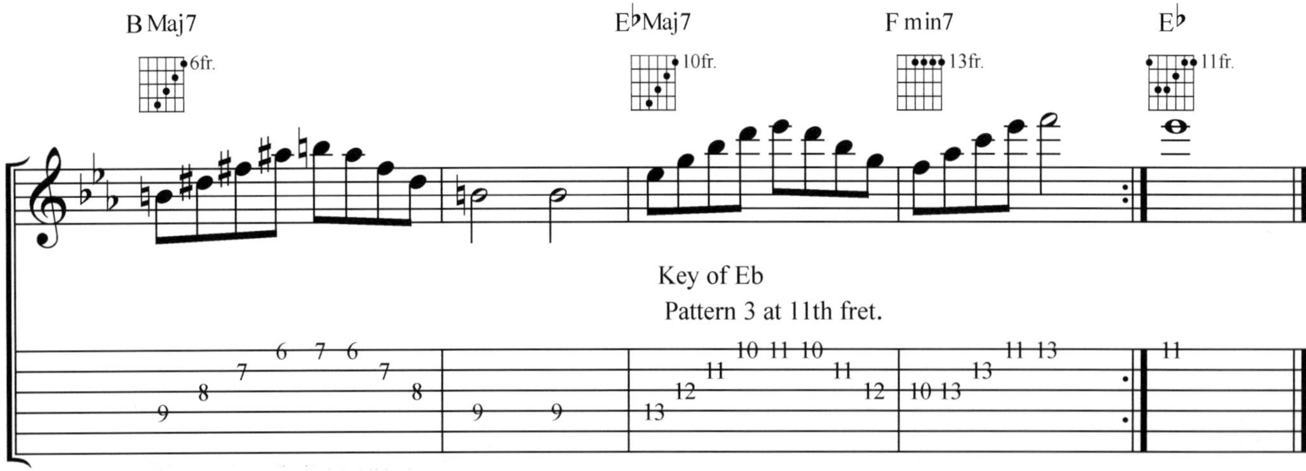

This common progression is written in the key of Eb (3 flats). However, there are implied key modulations (changes), as it borrows chords from other keys, i.e. Ebmin7 is the II chord of Db.

Finding Key Center
Arpeggio to Scale

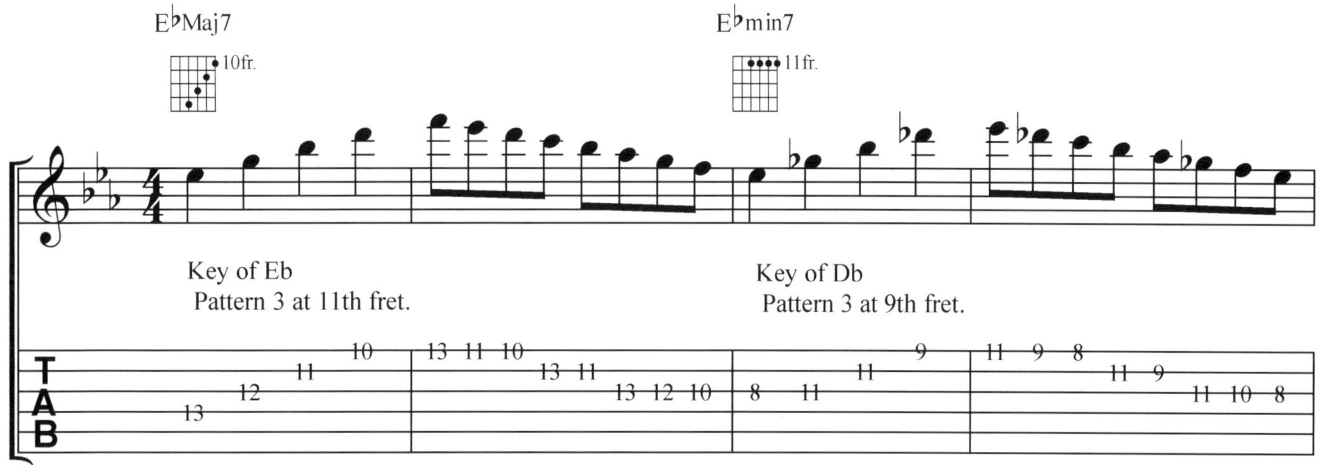

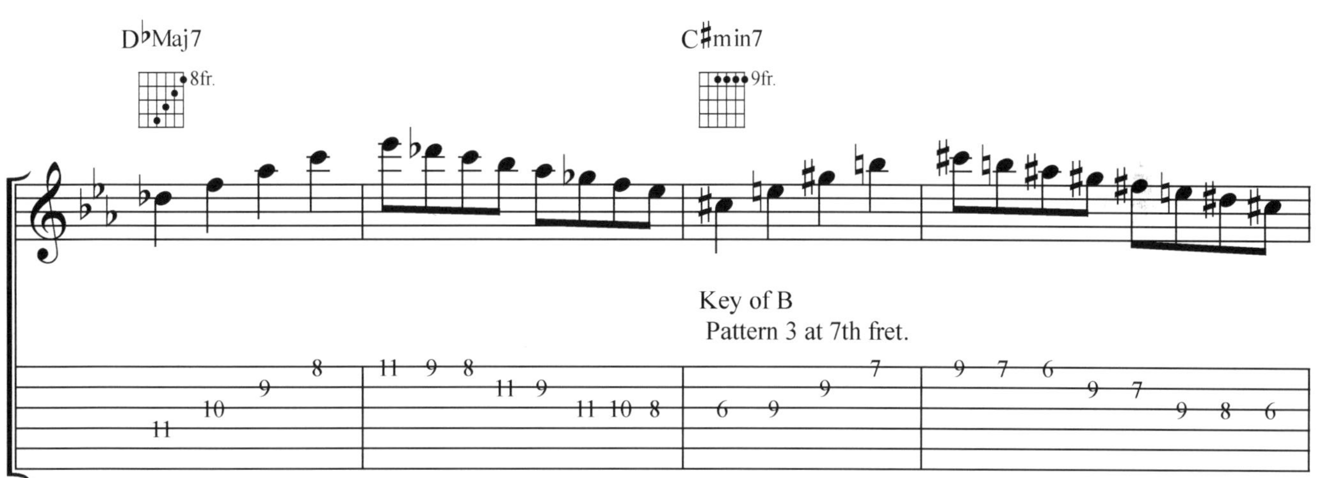

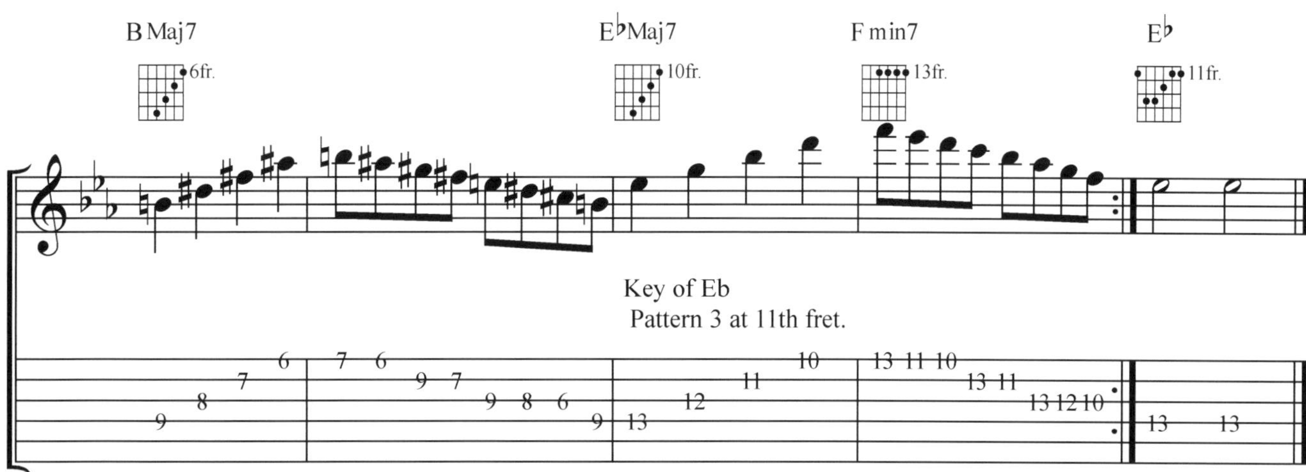

Finding Key Center
Arpeggio Study

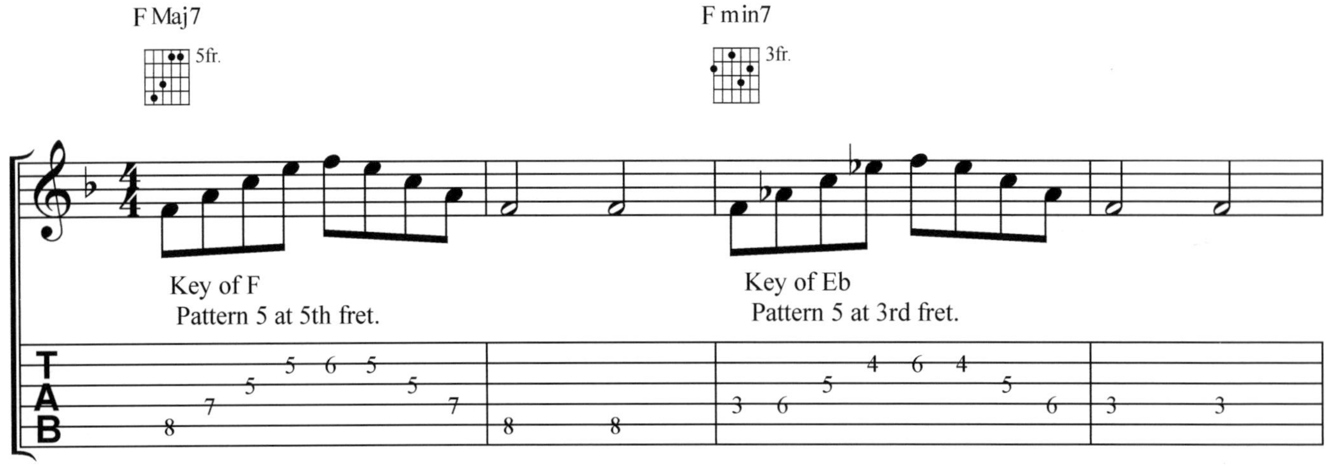

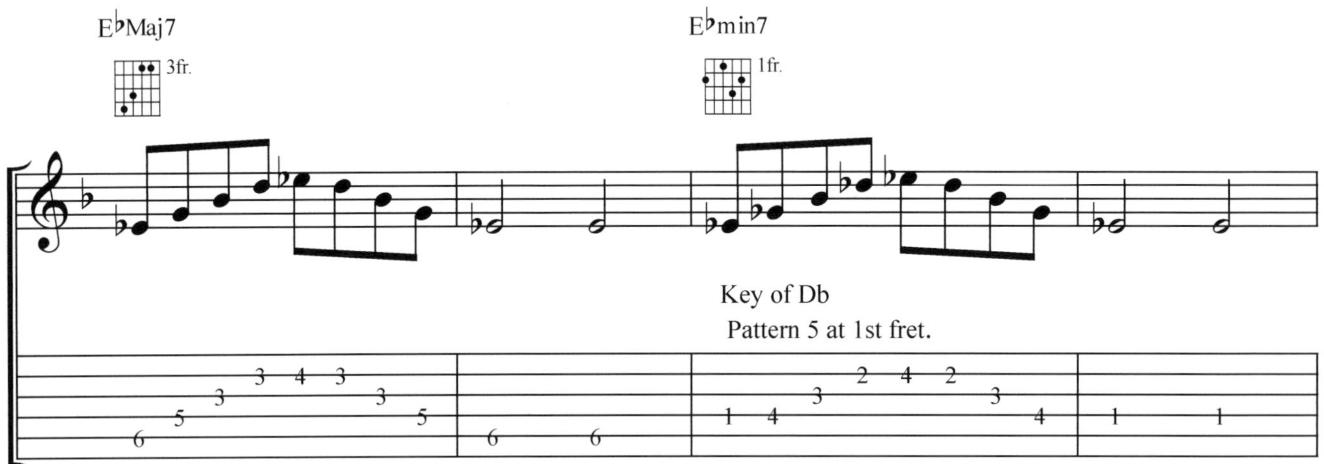

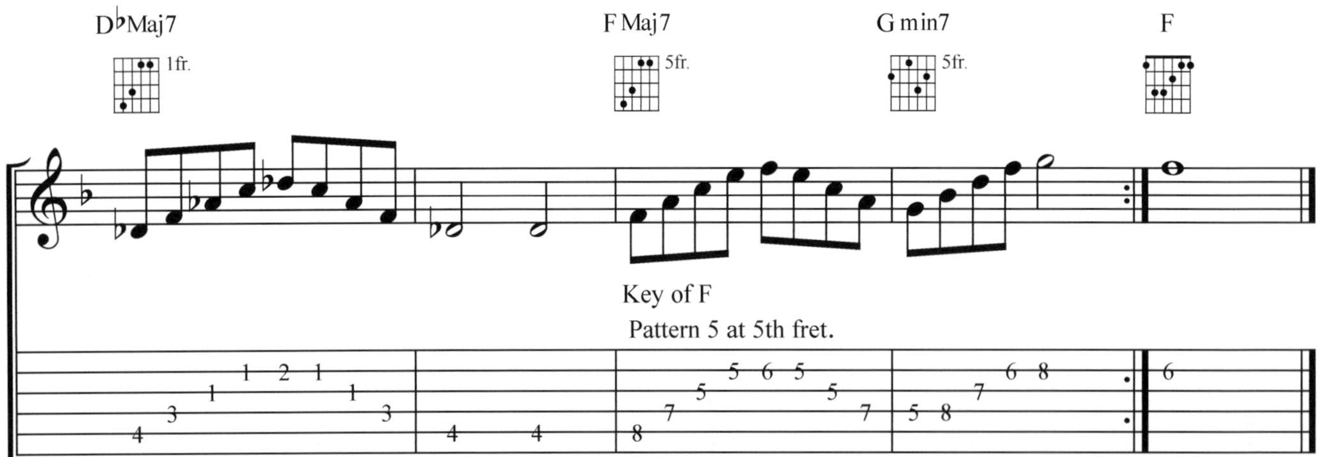

This common progression is written in the key of F (1 flat). However, there are implied key modulations (changes), as it borrows chords from other keys, i.e. Fmin7 is the II chord of Eb.

Finding Key Center
Arpeggio to Scale

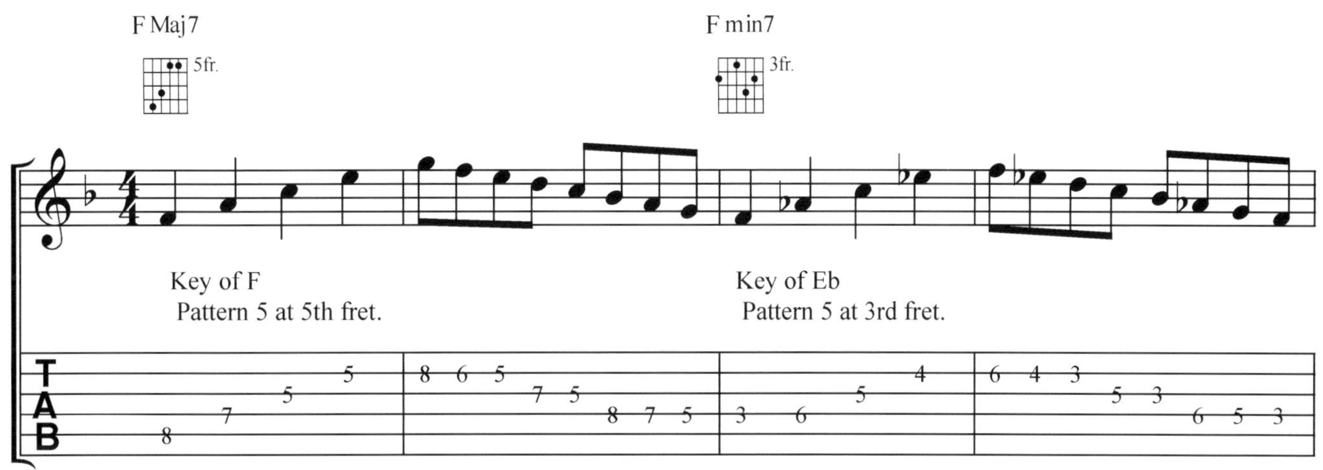

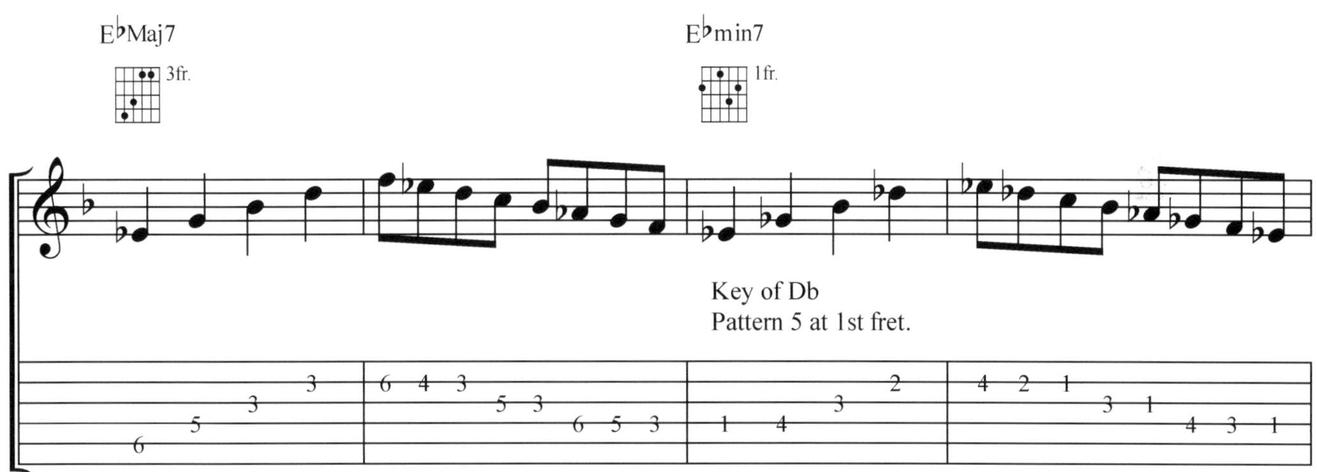

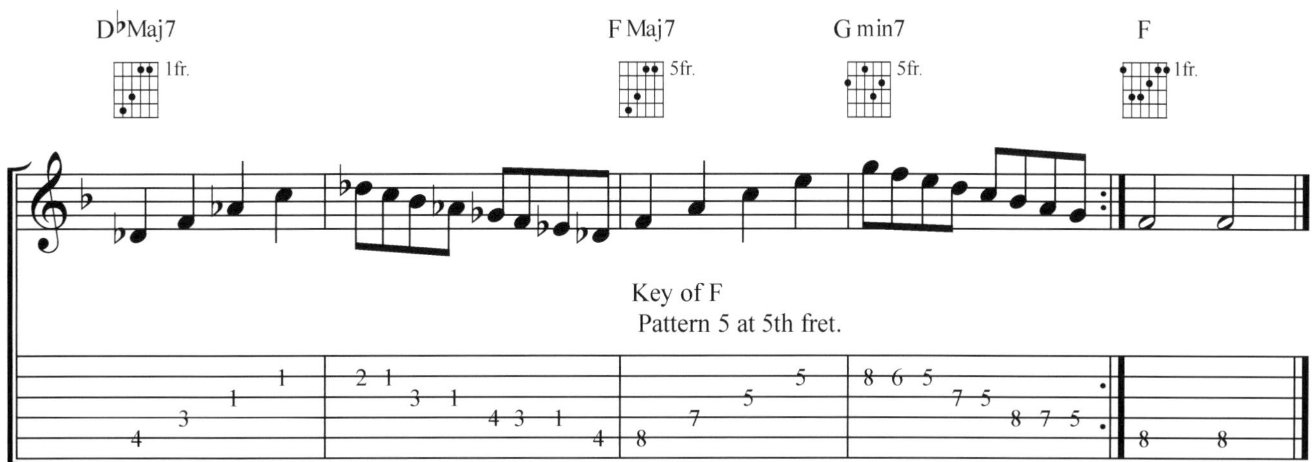

Finding Key Center
Arpeggio Study

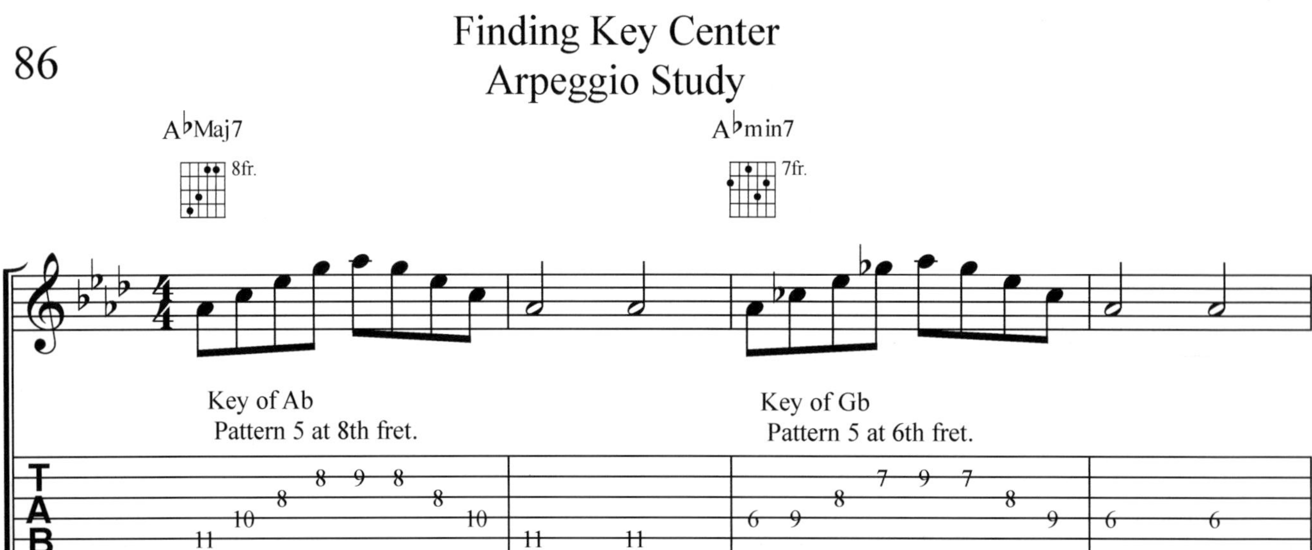

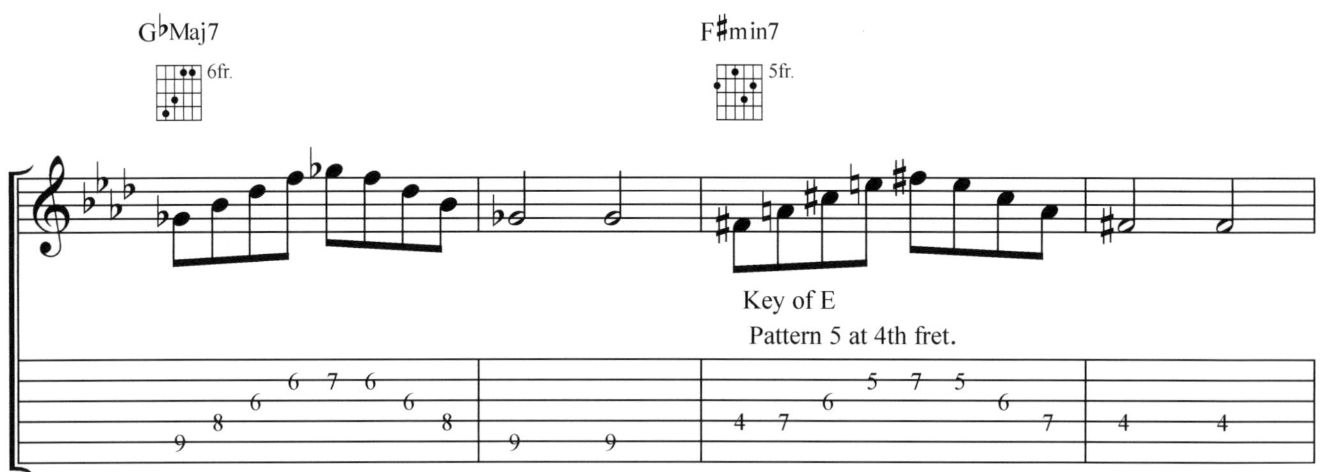

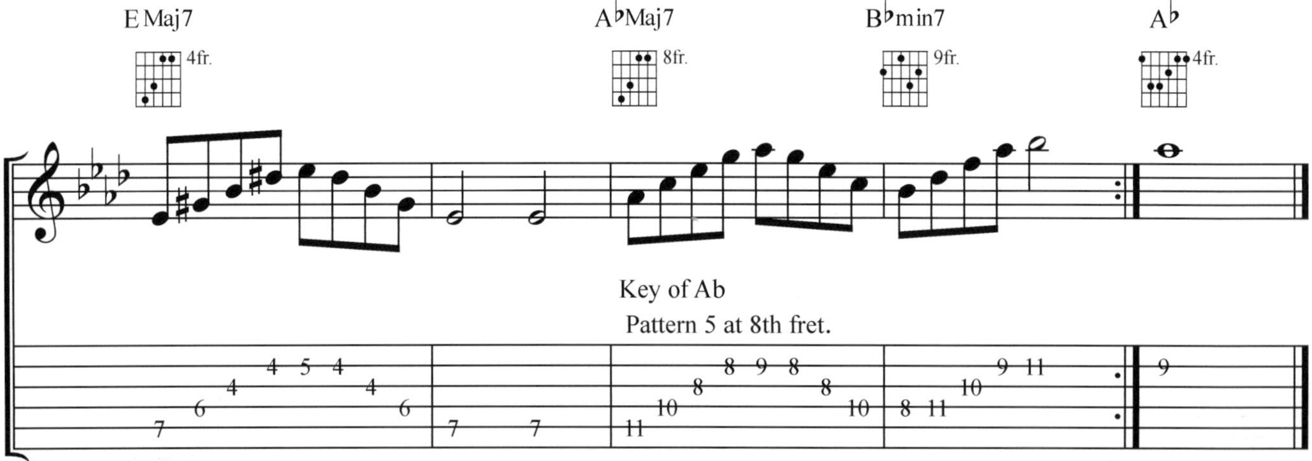

This common progression is written in the key of Ab (4 flats). However, there are implied key modulations (changes), as it borrows chords from other keys, i.e. Abmin7 is the II chord of Gb.

Finding Key Center
Arpeggio to Scale

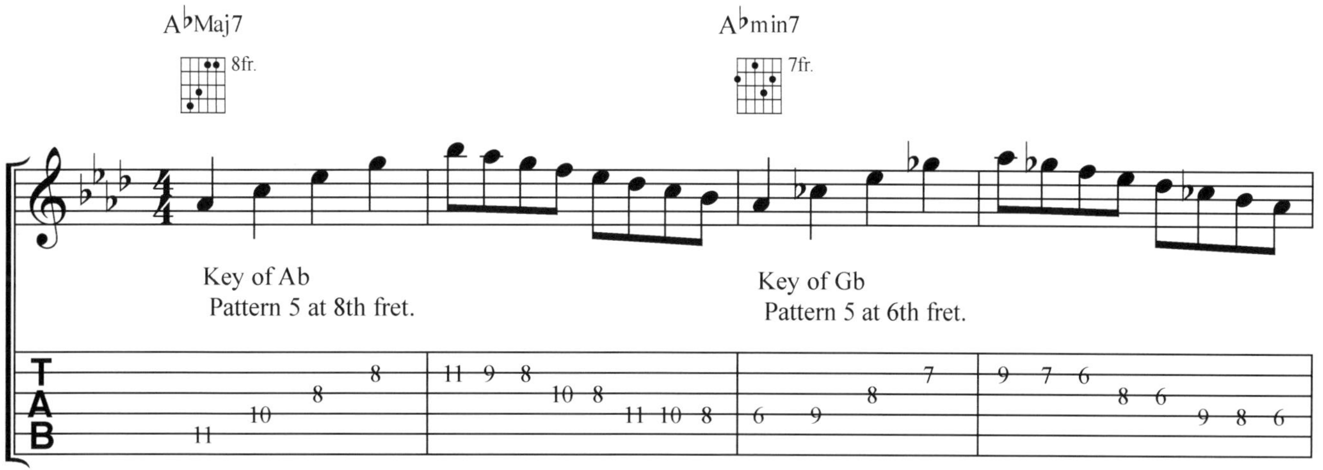

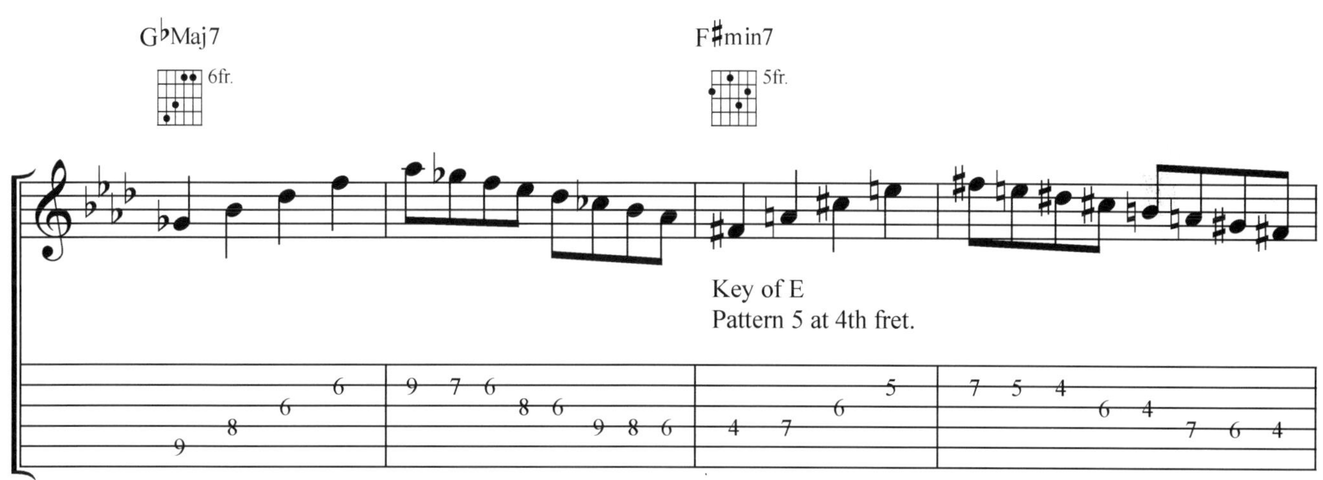

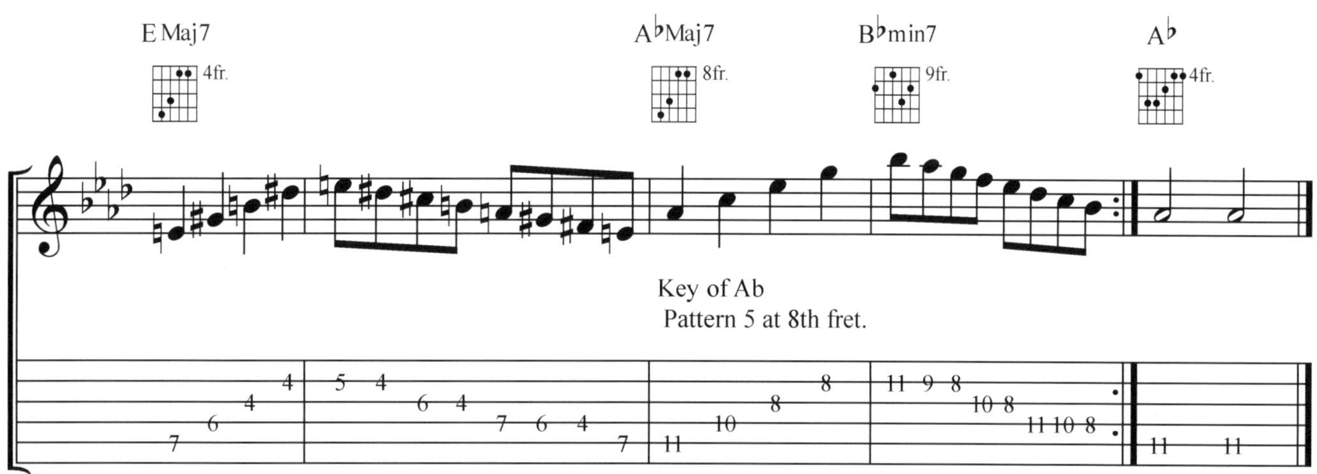

Made in the USA
Columbia, SC
27 July 2021